Maureen O'Carroll

*A Musical Memoir
of an
Irish Immigrant Childhood*

Maureen O'Carroll
and Leora O'Carroll

Foreword by Barry Tuckwell AC, OBE

For more information, please visit:
MaureenOCarroll.com

CONTENTS

In memory of
May Gahan O'Carroll

FOREWORD

In the early years of my life we moved constantly around Australia and New Zealand as my father, a Wurlitzer organist, played at movie theaters to support our family. When World War II began he joined the Royal Australian Air Force and I, along with my mother and sister Patricia, settled with our cousins in Neutral Bay on the lower North Shore area of Sydney. There I went to Homebush High but was soon so bored at school that I simply stopped going and was subsequently expelled for truancy.

As a young teenager I moved to the Conservatorium of Music High School, which is where I first met Maureen. She was around 11 years old and I immediately recognized her as someone with a fellow rebel spirit. The immense musical talent of the O'Carroll family was well known at the Conservatorium and I also got to know her sisters Patricia and Cathleen. However, my days at the school were limited as my delinquent ways managed to get me expelled again.

Fortunately the French Horn saved me from my wayward youth and while still a teenager, my music career was launched, taking me first to Melbourne, then back to Sydney and finally overseas to London. Later on during my solo career, I had the good fortune to meet up with Maureen many times, first in Australia when she was playing with the Sydney Symphony Orchestra and after that we met regularly for decades as our paths continued to cross both in the U.S. and Australia. Maureen exuded such *joie de vivre* and I continued to admire her and how she managed a career as a fine cellist as well as raising three children on her own. She always had a glint in her eye, possessing terrific wit and humour and, not infrequently, that rebel spirit I first saw in her as a girl, would show itself again.

It wasn't until I read this book about Maureen's childhood written by her and her daughter, Leora, that I fully appreciated how separate our lives were growing up in Sydney. Maureen was part of a large Irish Catholic family living in the blue collar area of Balmain. Sydney then was very segmented and us Church of Englanders were taught not to mix with the Catholics. Fortunately music brought us all together during our schools days at the Conservatorium, and ideas of segregation didn't cross our young minds.

This book brought back so many childhood memories of Depression-era Sydney. That familiar world is made enchanting in the book because of Maureen's humourous recollection of her unique upbringing in this quirky but ambitious large

Irish Immigrant family brimming with musical talent. There are many such stories in Australia's history, each one unique in their own way and Maureen's story and that of her family shows us how many ways there are to survive and flourish even when times are tough.

Maureen O' Carroll was a lifelong friend. She kept her rebel spirit throughout her life and I loved her for it.

Barry Tuckwell

Piper's Creek, Australia

FAREWELL

The letter arrived on Monday. It was addressed to me, but as the beige-colored envelope was typed and very official-looking with an overseas airmail stamp, my mother had opened it before I arrived home. From the New Zealand Broadcasting Service, it read:

> *You have been recommended for the position of 'cellist in the New Zealand National Orchestra by the conductor of the Sydney Symphony Orchestra, Mr. Eugene Goossens. We wish to offer you this position at the salary of ten pounds per week. Should you accept, arrangements have been made for your transportation with the Union Steam Ship Company on the 'Wanganui' sailing from Sydney to Wellington on August 22, 1950. A representative from the Service will meet you at the ship in Wellington on August 25th.*

I read the letter over and over again until I knew it by heart. I was being given three days notice to leave everything that I knew.

Bewildered, I turned to my mother and cried,

"I'm not ready! How can I possibly leave here in three days?" I handed the letter back to her. "How can I go alone to a strange country and play in a professional orchestra when I've never even been away from home!"

Mother turned a deaf ear to all of my protests. She had accepted the letter as a *fait accompli* and was already lifting stored garments and papers from a small, wood-bound fiber trunk that was part of our household furnishings, evaluating its potential to contain my worldly goods.

"If Mr. Goossens thinks you're ready, you're ready. You can't stay around here for the rest of your life. After all," she said, looking at me across the lid of the trunk, "you'll be eighteen in a couple of weeks. It's time to go out and work, and besides, you'll be able to send home five pounds a week to help with your brothers." The conversation was closed.

The next day, I saw my cello teacher, John Kennedy, at the Conservatorium of Music. I told him about the job offer. To my surprise, he was enthusiastic that I should accept it.

"You really must go" he said encouragingly. "It will give you a chance to find out what it's like to play in a professional orchestra. You can learn about living away from home, and look, you'll have a few quid in your pocket and that's always nice."

He opened a volume of music, placing it on the stand and continued with his paternal advice, "So, take the job for six months and then come back to me. By then you'll have a very good idea of the direction you want your playing to take."

The remainder of the lesson was spent working on orchestral excerpts for New Zealand and I stoically accepted the fact that in two days I would be sailing away from Sydney.

The trunk was packed. It contained my collection of music and my clothes which included a new skirt, two sets of "winter woolies" for the cold climate to which I was going, and a long black concert dress which had previously done service with my three older sisters.

On Thursday morning, I awoke feeling utterly bereft. My limbs wouldn't function and I felt that my body didn't have any bones in it.

I pleaded with my mother, "I can't possibly go. I feel terribly sick."

She was spooning out bowlfuls of porridge and hesitating in her task, looked at me somberly, "I do understand", she said with reserved compassion. "You'll be alright once you get something in your stomach."

We all sat at the kitchen table, unusually silent, my five younger brothers constantly taking quick glances at me over their raised spoons. For a moment, I caught the curious look of my youngest brother, eight year-old Peadar, and thought of what my mother had said about sending half of my wages home to help with the remaining children. She was now fifty, my father fifty-six, and on a very modest income they still had the responsibility of five boys under the age of eighteen to raise.

I was fifth in a family of ten children, all of whom displayed musical talent. My parents, in their ambitious determination to have us all become musicians, saw this profession as a path to a richer and more rewarding life-style than might be expected for children from a large Irish immigrant family. So for their teenage daughter to have been offered a position as cellist in a professional orchestra, and at the princely sum of ten pounds a week (when an average starting salary in the workforce was a fifth of that), must have made them proud.

The strained breakfast time finally ended and while we were clearing the table, my parents called me into their bedroom. My older sister Pat broke the tension with a giggled whisper. "I'll bet this is when you get that long overdue talk about sex." She wasn't far wrong.

I went into the bedroom and stood opposite my parents, their double bed separating us. My parent's bedroom was always sacrosanct, and was the one area of our small house where we would be invited only for serious discussions, the door firmly closed after we were admitted.

"Well," my father said, "you're going away from your home now. You know that we've done our best for you, and have always tried to keep you out of harm's way. But now you will be alone and making your own decisions, and remember that these will reflect on your family."

There was another long pause, while my mother stood silently next to him, watching me. I knew that they could never find the words with which to express themselves completely and I only wanted this painful moment to end. It did.

My father came towards me, affirming "We

know that you will be a good girl." He then gave me a short, painful hug and in a strained voice said "We have to hurry, the taxi will be here soon," and left the room, closing the door behind him.

My mother's hug was longer, accompanied by a whispered "God Bless You."

She then took from a string bag, long strips of heavy brown wrapping paper. "Now we don't want you getting sick on the boat, do we? Take off your jumper and skirt and I'll get you fixed up for the voyage" my mother instructed.

After I had undressed, she proceeded to bind my ribs and stomach with the long strips of brown paper, holding each one firmly against me, while on her command, I revolved slowly. As each strip was wound around me and a new one started, she reassured me, describing how effective this preventive measure had been when she had sailed to the colonies from Ireland.

"Your Aunt Josie was sick for the whole trip. Miserable she was. But I was right as rain because I had the good sense to listen to my Mam, and I wrapped brown paper around my stomach, but your Aunt wouldn't do it."

She chatted on, reminiscing about her sea voyage, maintaining a sense of normalcy, "When we all went out to New Zealand on the 'Rimutaka', I kept myself wrapped in the paper and even though the trip took seven weeks, I was never sick.

I even won the dance and the skipping rope competitions on board."

Finally she secured the last strip of paper with a heavy safety pin. I didn't know what seasickness was, but listening to my mother's advice, I had to assume that it was a lot worse than the rigid discomfort of being trussed up in wrapping paper. But I did wonder how she had managed to walk about, much less dance and skip rope. I dressed, and stiffly emerged from the bedroom, protectively parceled, now ready to be sent on my sea voyage – and out into the world.

We all stood by the open front door with the labeled trunk, watching for the taxi to appear over the hill. The family bowed their heads while my father recited the ecumenical prayer he always said with us every day before we left the house:

"Great Creator, hold us in Thy keeping,"

"This day and always, teach us right."

The large taxi pulled up to the front door. The trunk was put in the boot and we all squeezed in for the trip to the wharf at Pyrmont.

A noisy, gala atmosphere overwhelmed us at the crowded dockside. Passengers and guests milled about, exchanging squealed greetings with desperate gaiety, while poker-faced stewards tried vainly to keep the gang-plank clear. In the short time that I had had to prepare for this journey, I had fantasized about having a glamorous farewell like the ones in the movies. I would gracefully ascend the gang-plank, bouquet in arms, smiling, waving and throwing gentle kisses to everybody. But when the time came for me to board the ship, I could only, in my bound-up state, lumber awkwardly up the gang-plank, lugging my cello, followed by a nervous family.

The cabin I had been assigned was excitedly examined by all of us, the tiny bathroom admired, and the distances to the various decks paced out. We found our way to the dining room, and expressed astonishment at the length and variety of the menu and the large number of waiting stewards standing to attention in their smart white jackets.

Suddenly this inquisitive, happy activity was interrupted by the deep, woeful blast of the ship's horn and the announcement over the loud speaker – "All ashore who's going ashore."

I became immobilized knowing that the moment had come when I was about to be parted from my family and the life that I knew. But my parents had experienced painful farewells many times before and had learned how to handle them.

My father thrust into my hands a large packet of various colored streamers and instructed me in a comforting voice, "You'll soon see us down on the dock. Give us a wave and throw a streamer to each of us. But remember, make sure that you hold on to the ends." Then, in the confused and crowded atmosphere of the little cabin, we said hurried farewells and kissed, and my family was gone.

I found my way through the crowding passengers to the deck railing and there, standing below me on the busy dock, waving and smiling bravely, were my parents, and my brothers and sisters. In a moment of levity, I threw down one of the rolled streamers to each of them, while retaining the ends in my left hand. Then the ship's band, stationed on the deck, broke into the familiar "Maori Farewell" –

"Now is the hour that we must say good-bye.

Soon I'll be sailing across the sea..."

Deafened by the repeated blast of the ship's horn and blinded by uncontrollable tears, I leant over the railing, clutching my handful of streamers as the tug boats pulled the ship away from the dock. The blurred figures of my family grew smaller and as each streamer unrolled to its full length, it grew taut and snapped.

TO THE COLONIES

My mother, May Gahan, was born on Old Ship Street in Dublin, Ireland in 1899, one of six children. As a girl, she was given dancing lessons and in her early teens, was invited to join the dance troupe of the Abbey Theatre in Dublin. Through this association she became involved in the Irish Citizen Army, an underground organization whose goal was to remove British rule and gain independence for Ireland.

Fifteen year-old May worked as a runner for the Citizen Army, a responsibility which was often given to young women as they were less likely to arouse suspicion than male youths. In this capacity, she carried messages back and forth with information about maneuvers of British troops and munitions, clandestine meetings, and orders from the Irish leaders. She methodically set out to learn the location of every house and back alley in Dublin that would offer refuge and escape. This strategic knowledge, combined with her messenger skills and fearlessness, made her a valued member of the First Easter Division of the Irish Volunteers, and Cumann na Mban, the women's division of the Citizen Army. As one of very few women, she fought in the six-day 1916 Easter Rebellion, first at St. Stephen's Green, under the leadership of Countess Constance Markeivicz and then was sent as a messenger to the center of the fighting at the Dublin General Post Office, where defying the might of the British Army, the rebels raised the Irish tri-color and declared Ireland to be a Republic. After staying with the fighters for three days, she ventured from the Post Office and survived open gunfire to carry messages to other rebel headquarters. She was finally captured by British troops while helping wounded men who were hiding in the vaults at the Marlborough Street Cathedral.

With other captured rebels, May was taken to Richmond Barracks and then marched through the streets to Kilmainham Gaol. The rebellion at this stage was unpopular with the Irish people who feared further retribution from the British. On the way, the marching prisoners were jeered and pelted with horse dung and bottles.

May was put in a small cell with two other women. But as there was only one bed, two of them took turns standing while the other slept. During the next two weeks, as the men who had led the rebellion were taken out one by one and shot by the British, their sympathetic jailer each time climbed to the barred window of the women's cell to solemnly inform them as to who the latest victim was, remarking "Well, another one's gone."

Finally came the time when he had to tell them that James Connolly, their leader, who had been badly injured in the leg, was taken from his hospital bed at Dublin Castle, and unable to stand, had faced the firing squad – the last of the rebels to be shot – strapped into a wheelchair.

Three of May's four brothers were also members of the Citizen Army and in the midst of preparations for the rebellion, they had brought home a young recruit who had come to Dublin from Waterford, and introduced him to their sister. His name was John O'Carroll.

For their efforts in the Easter Uprising, my father and one of May's brothers were housed in Mountjoy Gaol. The other two Gahan brothers, Matt and Joe, were deported to prison in England. As no social services were available for their families, May collected coins to help them by standing at Nelson's Column on O'Connell Street extending a heavy metal can by its handle. A policeman named Johnny Barton approached her, "May, you know it's against the law to collect funds for prisoners."

"My brothers have been wrongly gaoled" she protested, "and I won't let their families starve."

Reaching for the can, the policeman ordered,

"Well, you're not going to do your collecting here on the main street of Dublin."

May pulled away and swung at him with the heavy can. Johnny Barton, unconscious and with his head bleeding, was taken to hospital. My mother was again taken to Kilmainham Gaol.

* * *

Because of the execution of the fifteen leaders of the Easter Rebellion, by the time the last of the rebels were released from gaol in 1917, the tide of public opinion had turned in their favor and the leaders were now regarded as martyrs, and the rebels, heroes.

That same year, on May 8th, May Gahan and John O'Carroll were married in Dublin. When their daughter was born a year later, they named her Eileen Markievicz, in honor of Countess Markievicz. They then had a son, Robert Emmett, named for the beloved leader of the brief 1803 rebellion. For the next five years, May's parents assumed the responsibility of raising the two children as the young couple continued to fight for Irish independence, and were frequently imprisoned for their involvement in the Anglo-Irish War (1919-20); the Black and Tans (1920-21); and the Irish Civil War (1922-23).

However, the years of periodic internment, hunger strikes in the gaols and the subsequent brutal force feedings, the stress of illicit political activities and what my mother often referred to as "waiting for the knock on the door", all took their toll on her health. She and my father had given a lot of their youth to the Irish cause and after the unsatisfactory compromise of Partition and the devastating Civil War that followed, along with the poor economic conditions in Ireland, a decision was made in 1925 to leave the 'old country' to make a fresh start, and hopefully renew my mother's health, in the colonies. They chose New Zealand.

❈ ❈ ❈

John O'Carroll went ahead of his family, securing a passage as a steward on the ship, the "Hokitika". Shortly thereafter, the family followed – his wife May, her younger brothers Robert and John, her sister Josephine ("Josie"), the two children, Eileen and Emmett and May's parents, who had raised their grandchildren thus far and did not want to be separated from them.

The family settled in Auckland and found in New Zealand the temperate climate they had sought for my mother's health, but initially the strangeness of the country overwhelmed them. Never before had they encountered such striking-looking people as the indigenous New Zealanders, the Maoris, many of whom had their faces elaborately tattooed. The young country was sparsely settled and the unaccustomed quiet was often interrupted by peculiar bird calls, unlike any they had ever heard before.

Their brick terrace house fronting a crowded Dublin street was now replaced with a timber home surrounded by spacious grounds with a garden that grew exotic flora. Ferns and palms, which in the old country had been cultivated only as parlor plants, grew in profusion in their backyard as did tangled flowering vines. Many yards also had a lemon or orange tree, and these fruits that in Ireland were imported and expensive, were now "free for the picking". The butcher shops sold half a lamb for only a few shillings and the markets offered an extraordinary variety of reasonable and fresh foods. The immigrant family adventurously sampled some of these new delicacies, puckering at the astringent bitterness of the ruby-colored tamarillo but relishing the sweetness of the fuzzy Chinese gooseberry.

New Zealand appeared to offer them the secure

and comfortable life they had envisioned. Jobs were found for the adults and schools for the children who were also able to continue their music studies. A baby girl was born, Cathleen Clare, a sister to Eileen and Emmett, now eleven and ten.

However, a gradual shift from their initial excitement occurred for a variety of reasons. May's beloved mother, Eileen, died unexpectedly at age fifty-one of peritonitis, and her bereaved husband decided to return home to Ireland, taking with him his son, Robert. Aunty Josie then married and moved away to her own home and so the family was quickly reduced to John and May O'Carroll, their three children and Uncle John.

As Irish Catholics, in a country that proved to be imperialistic and predominantly Protestant, they were in the minority, and although my parents had obtained jobs, with increasing evidence of a depression, they feared losing them. In addition, they experienced several strong earth tremors. Though they were aware that New Zealand was prone to earthquakes, the reality of these shocking tremors and then the occurrence of a major quake in 1929 (measuring 7.6 on the Richter scale), terrified them.

Australia, a larger and more populous country that also welcomed immigrants, was a voyage of only a few days across the Tasman Sea. John and May debated the pros and cons of gambling on yet another uprooting of their lives, but finally, possessions were packed and passage on the "Wanganella" was booked. The family of six, now without the support system of any relatives, but with nervous optimism for their future in this new country, sailed into Sydney Harbor in March, 1930.

* * *

Balmain, a peninsula area of Sydney, washed on three sides by the inner harbor, was where the O'Carrolls found a house to rent. It was a free-standing brick terrace, built in 1861, and not dissimilar to May's childhood home in Dublin. Located at 220 Darling Street, it was on the main thoroughfare of this crowded, working-class neighborhood. The family was happy to be in a bigger city and an area that had a large Irish population.

The house had a shop in the front, and my father, with Uncle John, now a barber, set up a hairdressing salon and tobacconist. Symbolic of the end of their travels and settlement in Australia, my father named it "The Anchor".

The family worked hard at building their new life, but had arrived in Sydney in the midst of the Depression, and their immigrant journeys had exhausted any savings. The reality of their tenuous situation became all too clear when the landlord announced that he was going to sell the house, and knowing that his sale would be easier if the large family moved out and the home could be offered with vacant possession, gave them one month's notice. The only option for remaining at 220 Darling Street was to purchase the house with a deposit of one hundred pounds, an unattainable amount of money.

This threat to the fragile stability of their household particularly upset May. She had now given birth to a fourth child, Patricia Josephine, and was aware of how difficult it would be to find affordable housing for a large family, and knew that having to move would ruin the business they were establishing.

Every morning, May, a small compact woman no taller than five foot two, dressed in her best outfit, put her two infant girls in the large perambulator, and walked to any address that was advertised for rent, evaluating its feasibility to house her family of seven. She returned home each afternoon, more dispirited and increasingly afraid for their future.

One day May stopped to view a tiny cottage on Edward Street that was up for rent, but standing on the worn sandstone step marking its narrow entrance, she could assess that it was impossible to consider housing a family in this small dwelling. With a heavy heart, she turned around, pushed the pram the short distance to Thornton Park, and wearily sat on a bench.

Repeatedly bouncing the handle of the carriage up and down to sooth the babies, she gazed across the water, her eyes fixed on the great arch of the almost completed bridge which spanned the massive harbor into which she had sailed with such hope, only a couple of years before. She remembered wistfully that a photographer on the dock, drawn to her vivacious smile and elegant appearance as she waved in excitement, had taken her photograph. Her pretty face, framed by curly dark brown hair bobbed in the fashion of the day, had a generous smile, gray-blue eyes that flashed readily and a translucent Celtic skin of which she was proud and protected from the harsh Australian sun with brimmed hats.

The photographer had sent her a copy of the photo and it was now framed and placed on the bedroom bureau as a reminder of her hopes and dreams.

Still rocking the carriage, her weary eyes filled with tears and she surrendered her optimism and wept. A gentle arm squeezing her shoulder startled her, "Come on love, what would make a young mother weep her heart out like this? What is so terrible?" And May, with no mother of her own, found herself in the comforting arms of an older woman, and between sobs, explained her desperate situation.

"We're to lose the house and the business" she cried "and we have nowhere to go. We've worked so hard to get ahead but it's hopeless." May paused, "Just hopeless. I was so sure that we could make a go of it here, but now we might even be put out on the street."

For an Irish person raised with family accounts of the Potato Famine, the idea of eviction was particularly terrifying. Patting May's shoulder, the older woman sat quietly, watching her and continued listening.

"Here we are with four children to feed and clothe" my mother sighed, "and now I'm expecting another baby."

Mrs. Delores, for that was the kind woman's name, heard the rest of May's story and waiting patiently until the young mother's weeping had stopped, gently asked more questions about the family and the business. She nodded in contemplation, was quiet for a while, then finally looked at May decisively and said "I believe there's a reason why I came to this park today. I'm a widow now, with my own little house. I only have one child and she is almost grown up." She took my mother's hand "I've got a bit of money set aside... And I'm going to lend you the hundred pounds to buy that house."

Because of Mrs. Delores' extraordinary generosity and intuitive faith, 220 Darling Street became the O'Carroll's home, and true to the name my father gave it, the business became the family's anchor. Over time, the debt was repaid and Mrs. Delores remained a respected and loved friend who witnessed the growth and successes of the family.

Six months after the providential meeting between the two women, in September of 1932, I was born in the upstairs bedroom and named Maureen Cyril.

ORCHESTRA OF THE ELVES

Though it may be a mystery as to how our memory orders the sequence of events in our lives, music making was ever-present in our household during my childhood, so perhaps it could be expected then, that my earliest memories are associated with music.

What is the evocative power of an object, a phrase, an aroma or a melody, that it can tap into our subconscious and suddenly lay memories of our past, our childhood, before us?

Later in life, I visited my dear friend Brian Duke who had been my stand partner in the Sydney Symphony Orchestra. With pride, he displayed his latest addition to his antique collection. It was a wind-up gramophone. He took a new steel needle from a small tin box, and, securing it in the arm, placed a recording of Strauss Waltzes on the turntable to demonstrate for me how this old-style machine operated. As I gazed at the revolving black disc and listened to the crackling sounds of these familiar melodies, a carousel of memories turned and turned.

* * *

Professor Sauer, a stooped European man with a shock of grey hair, was a music maker. He conducted his own orchestra of young people and they gave frequent performances in the small Palings Concert Hall in Sydney. For these occasions, the girls in the orchestra wore blue pleated skirts with white satin blouses and the boys, powder blue trousers and smart cropped jackets of blue and white linen. The music program was selected to please the proud parents who supported this student orchestra, and included such works as Strauss Waltzes, Brahms Hungarian Dances and various popular overtures.

My brother, Emmett, thirteen years my senior, played violin in "Professor Sauer's Young People's Orchestra" as a teenager. Sometimes my mother took me to these performances but not before a pre-concert lecture to her three year-old about not fidgeting, not talking and not demanding trips to the toilet while the orchestra was playing. I loved going to these concerts but while I readily agreed to her rules, they were just as readily ignored. On more than one occasion while the music was playing, I was hurried out of the hall and in the privacy of the empty lobby, given a smack. The smacks were quickly forgotten but the sights and sounds of the orchestra remained with me.

At about the same time, our family acquired a gramophone. The box was magical. It had a round disc on top with an arm that swung out and on one side was a wind-up crank. The front of the box had two little wooden doors with round knobs, and behind them, with the sound coming from it, was a shiny brass chute which disappeared into the box. I was fascinated with the echo-like noise of the music and loved playing with the doors, opening and closing them to make the sound louder and softer. But I was puzzled. I had only ever heard music performed live, with the players visible, and couldn't figure out who could be making this music.

I asked my brother Emmett about this mystery because he was big and he knew everything. He carefully explained to me that at the bottom of the brass chute lived a band of elves who could all play musical instruments. When the gramophone was wound up, it rang a bell inside and the elves would quickly pick up their little violins, cellos, and trumpets, jump into their tiny chairs, and start playing.

If only I could see those elves! In story books, they were always pictured in little green suits and pointy shoes, but this was an orchestra of elves, so I knew they would be sitting together in powder blue outfits playing their tiny violins, with a grey-haired elf in a black coat conducting them. I desperately wanted one of my own – a musical elf to play with and to carry about in my pocket.

One day when no one was about, I crept up to the gramophone, opened the doors and with my hand, very carefully reached down the brass chute. Leaning against the box with my shoulder I blindly, but gently, patted around trying to locate an elf. My groping hand felt a piece of metal shift and I wondered if I had knocked over the elves' bell. Then my fingers touched something very soft and round. I had found an elf! He was furry. I could also feel a little stick, and decided that he must be holding his violin bow. I stretched my arm to the limit and managed to gently pick him up with my thumb and forefinger, and cautiously lifted him up and out of the chute.

To my horror, I wasn't holding an elf at all, but a furry grey dust ball with some tiny twigs embedded in it! Still not prepared to accept defeat, I peeled off the outer layer just in case there was an elf inside this cocoon, but alas, it was all nothing but fuzzy bits of dust. I was now puzzled and dispirited and abandoned my search for the elves.

Later, my father went to play the gramophone and wound up the crank, but there was no sound. He kept jiggling it, and peered down the chute – "What's wrong with this machine, it's not working!" Continuing his futile adjustments he yelled out – "Who's been fooling with the gramophone? I can't get it to play!"

I silently watched my father, knowing that all of his jiggling wouldn't make the gramophone work, but I was too scared to tell him the terrible thing that I had done. Sorrowfully, I now knew that by having invaded their home, I had scared all the elves away, and the little orchestra would never play again.

UNWANTED & UNLOVED

Though I was a strong and healthy child, the sister born two years before me, Patricia, was premature, and her delicate health required much attention and energy from my mother. By the time I was four, our family had grown with the addition of three boys, Seamus, Sean and Liam, each born a year apart. Thus, being positioned in between a fragile older sister and three demanding baby boys, my sequence in the family order didn't allow me as much parental attention as I wanted, and like many middle children in larger families, I was convinced that I had been short-changed in the pecking order.

Top L- R: Eileen, May, Sean, Emmett, John, Seamus
Bottom L-R: Cathleen, Maureen, Patricia

And so in my childhood fantasies, I thought about a richer material life than I had been born into, the luxury of privacy and most importantly, the different ways in which I could attract my parent's undivided attention. With my introduction to Catholic schooling, I found what I decided was the ideal way to gain that attention.

The day came when my mother, possibly when I was underfoot one time too many, decided that it was my turn to join the scholars at St. Augustine's, the local Catholic school. Undoubtedly overwhelmed by the demands of eight children, she didn't enroll me in school in the traditional fashion – that is, taking me at the appropriate age and time of year to be registered and intro-duced to teachers. Instead, with exasperation, she exclaimed to my older sister, Cathleen, "Here, it's about time your sister went to school. She can go there with you this morning."

Escorted by my sister I was ushered into a class-room where the nun, garbed in black robes, her face youthened by a girdling wimple, promptly exclaimed "Take that child home! She's not old enough for school yet."

Cathleen's obedient efforts at following the nun's instructions were thwarted by my mother's determination to have me start school. After sev-eral days of being brought back and forth, and terse messages being replayed between the school and my mother, the defeated nun finally assigned me a desk and slate.

My excitement at being one of the "big girls" and starting school soon turned into disappoint-ment. As I hadn't started at the beginning of term, I didn't know the other children or the school rou-tine, nor was I prepared for the discipline required to sit still and pay attention for extended periods of time. So I was relieved when we were finally dis-missed after this long day and I could get my sister to take me home. My teacher pointed me in the direction of Cathleen's classroom, where I stood meekly in the doorway. Class was still in progress and the nun expressed annoyance at the interrup-tion – "Well, what do you want?"

"I want my big sister."

"I'm teaching. You can't disturb my class!"

Not knowing what to do, I nervously remained standing there. Impatiently, she waved her arm, the movement enunciated by the sound of her rosary jingling, and curtly said "Well then Miss, sit over there and wait."

From the doorway, this flourish appeared to gesture towards the floor under her desk. So, under the desk I crawled and squatted there, trying to make myself as inconspicuous as possible. Snickering started. As the giggling increased, the nun, with eraser in hand, turned from the blackboard to look for the cause of this disturbance. Peering down at me, she demanded "What are you doing under there, you little dunce!"

"You told me to sit here" I whimpered.

"I certainly did not!" the nun denied.

By now everybody was thoroughly enjoying this diversion, laughing unabashedly. That is, everybody except my mortified sister, the impatient teacher and me, a sobbing child curled up in a ball under the desk wondering how she could ever cope with this new life called "School".

I did cope. In fact, after my initial experience and adjusting to the new routine, I enjoyed school and looked forward to going there each day.

St. Augustine's also offered my first structured religious education and I was entranced with this pervasive aspect of my schooling: the exciting events of the Bible stories read to us, the physical beauty of the church, and the colorful theater of its ceremonies.

Each morning, the nun marched us in rows of twos from the classroom, across the small playground, to pray in the church. Upon entering, I would be comforted by the insulating quiet of the building and the appealing perfume of woody incense mingled with the honest, ever-present aroma of beeswax, with which the volunteer ladies of the church constantly burnished the wooden pews and doors. My eyes were always drawn to the shafts of tinted light shining through the stained glass windows highlighting the life-size religious statues. On the walls of St. Augustine's were the first paintings I ever saw, the fourteen dramatic depictions of the Stations of the Cross. And my introduction to Death was the large fascinating crucifix mounted on the wall by the church entrance – a ceramic representation of a naked Jesus outstretched on the Cross.

While I responded well to the structure of church and school life, where my efforts were acknowledged and I was often praised, I felt that I received very little of this recognition in my own disordered and crowded home, and interpreted this to mean that I was unwanted and unloved.

Once I became fixed on this notion, it was easy for me to read every criticism that my parents leveled at me as further proof that they didn't care about me.

One evening when I was again reprimanded for misbehaving and sent up to bed, I thought "I'll show them. They'll be really sorry now that I'm dead."

My five year-old concept of death was still the crucifix from St. Augustine's – Jesus nailed to the Cross. So I understood that when you died, you were naked, with closed eyes, outstretched arms and crossed feet.

I took off all of my clothes and then crept down to the landing of our staircase where I lay down, spread my arms, crossed my feet, and turned my head to the side, assuming the appropriate pose that Jesus had on the Cross. I didn't have a crown of thorns to put on my head, but that was okay.

I lay there waiting to be discovered, envisioning what would happen. My parents would stumble over my body and cry out "Oh no, she's dead! This happened because we treated her so badly." Weeping, they would promise, "If only she was alive, we would do anything for her. We would love her and spoil her because she deserves it more than any of her brothers and sisters."

I waited and waited and waited. The linoleum-covered floor was cold and I felt miserable, but despite my discomfort I eventually fell asleep. My father's angry voice awakened me - "This girl is absolutely impossible. What are we going to do with her!"

I opened my eyes to see both parents staring down at me in disbelief.

"But you don't understand" I cried in frustration.

It was obvious to me that my parents lacked the religious education that I had received at St. Augustine's. Still maintaining my Jesus pose, I insisted "Can't you see that I'm dead! I'm DEAD!"

MY FIRST CELLO

"Old Judge" was a brand of inexpensive plum jam that our family purchased in industrial-sized tins. Slightly rusty, and with the label removed, one of these empty tins was a favorite possession of mine when I was very little. One could feel important carrying about such an object. It could be placed on the head like a helmet, or used to hold precious treasures. Struck with a stick, it made a wonderful clanging sound and was always available as a ready stool. A lot of uses could be found for an empty ten-pound jam tin.

My brother Emmett, when not playing his violin, kept it under the bed in his room. I loved my big brother, but I loved his violin even more, and though I was constantly forbidden by him to go near it, the lure of the instrument was too great for me to heed his warnings. Waiting patiently with tin in hand until he left the house, I would sneak into his room, pull out his violin, perch it on my handy tin, excitedly balance his bow on the strings, and play it like a cello.

The care with which I took out his violin was

not exercised when returning it to the case and pushing it back under the bed. When Emmett came home and discovered my evident trespass, I would invariably hear the fateful words, "Where is she?" He would quickly find me and yell in frustration and anger - "I've told you to leave my violin alone. You stay away from my violin!"

Then he'd continue with my mother "Nothing is safe in this house. You've got to keep her away from my violin!"

Fortunately for me, my mother didn't seem to regard my transgression to be as serious as my brother did, "Now look, Emmett, she's only little and she's not hurting anything. You're sixteen years old, you should be able to keep your violin out of her way."

These confrontations continued as did my determination to have a real cello. I didn't want to play a violin under my chin like my brother and sister, Cathleen. We had a piano but the black and white keys didn't attract me. My sister Eileen played the harp but I was never tempted even to run my fingers up and down the strings. I wanted a cello.

For what seemed to be years, my parents placated me with, "One of these birthdays, you'll get a cello."

Finally, on my sixth birthday, I was taken alone by my father into the city. First, we went to

Woolworths where he bought me a black topsy doll, which I had always wanted. Then I walked up Hunter Street with Dad to the establishment of A.E. Smith, the prominent violin maker and dealer. Shiny violins were suspended from racks on the walls while a large glass case displayed bows of all shapes. Instrument cases were lying about and the shop had a warm smell of varnish and rosin. A bald elderly man in a grey linen apron emerged from the back room holding by the neck, a quarter-size cello.

"You're a lucky little girl" said A.E. Smith. "I chose this cello just for you."

I proudly marched out with Topsy in one arm and my new cello under the other. Dad wanted to carry it for me, but I wouldn't let him. Dodging other pedestrians, I struggled along Hunter Street and then we took the long walk to the ferry at the end of Erskine Street, passing a pub in every block. Beery drinkers standing outside the hotels with their schooners, good-naturedly called out to me - "Hey little girl, are you going to put that giant fiddle under your chin and give us a tune?"

I was frightened that one of them might take my cello from me, but was still determined to carry it onto the ferry all by myself. I noticed that other passengers were watching me sit with Topsy and my cello and even though they were smiling, I knew that they really envied me. Although Topsy was later betrayed in the most cruel fashion, this first cello remained my prized possession.

* * *

Now that I had an instrument, I was taken to the State Conservatorium of Music where at one time or another, all of the O'Carroll children studied. My cello teacher was Mr. William Ewart Gladstone Bell, otherwise known as "Gladdy". With such a formal name he was surely either related to Queen Victoria's Prime Minister or had cruel parents. So I began cello and studied with Gladdy for one nine-week term and in this time, I learned to hold the cello and acquired a concept of how to draw the bow and place my hand on the fingerboard.

However, finances in our household were always strained, and paying for music lessons was often a problem. We discovered under our parents' mattress, a drawstring bag containing coins of small denomination, and found out that this was money Mum had saved for music lessons. At one stage, the contents much have been too sparse to cover these expenses because our lessons at the Conservatorium ceased, and we were sent instead to the local Balmain Convent, The Convent of the Immaculate Conception, where the nuns gave music lessons for a nominal fee. My mother had inquired if they taught cello and of course they did.

They would have taught Hindustani if you paid them. They already taught violin, singing, piano, and now they were about to teach cello.

Sister Marcellus was my assigned teacher and asked me to play for her. But as I sat at the cello and drew the bow across the strings, she threw her hands up in the air, and an expression of horror appeared on her face.

"What a dreadful way for a young lady to sit!" she gasped, looking at me straddling the cello. "Who taught you to hold an instrument like that?"

Had I been more worldly, I would have realized that Sister had never seen a cello before.

"Mr. Bell taught me." I replied.

"I should have known. It was a man!"

She proceeded to have me sit in a "ladylike" side-saddle position with my legs crossed to one side and the cello perched against my hip. "Now sit back in the chair and make yourself comfortable, dear."

For six months, I had lessons at the convent in the early morning with Sister Marcellus and loved the attentive and caring experience. Every Monday and Thursday she greeted me with a hot cup of sugary tea, a biscuit, and a little snippet of wisdom such as "If you take a long drink of cold water first thing in the morning, you will have red lips."

Generally, I followed her advice though I never understood what these suggestions had to do with playing the cello. The lesson, after our initial chat, consisted of her humming melodies which were invariably hymns, while I played them by ear on the cello. Everything Sister Marcellus taught me was contrary to the most basic cello principles, but she was always kind, undemanding and encouraging.

However, my mother was astute enough to realize that even though I was enjoying these lessons, I was learning little. I suspect she also had the deep-seated Irish fear of a daughter being attracted to Convent Life.

I don't know if I returned to the Conservatorium because fees were paid or because Mother was persuasive with the administrators, but Gladdy was pleased to see me again, "How wonderful that you continued your cello. Now, suppose you play something for me and let me see what you can do."

The sight of his former student imperiously leaning back in the chair, seated side-saddle and clutching the bow like a club while she scraped away at "Faith of Our Fathers" left him staring and slack-jawed.

"I just can't believe this" he uttered. "It's... It's absolutely unbelievable. Wait here."

Gladdy left the room and shortly returned with three of the other music professors. As they

44

crowded into the small studio, he said "I want you all to see this – you are not going to believe it."

He turned to me, "Maureen, would you play for these gentlemen, please."

By now I was filled with a confidence such as I had never experienced before…. or since. Draping one leg over the other, I resumed my unique playing position and with great aplomb, sawed away at yet another hymn.

The professors turned to each other incredulously "I've heard about things like this but I never thought I'd actually see it."

I realized then that I really WAS a genius. I was deciding on which hymn to favor them with as an encore, when, much to my bewilderment, the audience shuffled out of the studio, shaking their heads. Then the bubble burst.

Mr. Bell looked at me with resignation, "I'm sorry, there is absolutely no way I can teach you. I wouldn't know where to start. Pack up and go home."

Utterly crushed, I set out on the long trip to Balmain. First, I dawdled through the Botanical Gardens and by the time I emerged at the Shakespeare statue at Macquarie Street, my cello had become heavy and I was tear stricken. I walked past the Colonial buildings that lined the street – the Mint, the Rum Hospital and the Houses of Parliament –

and then waited at the top of King Street for the tram that would take me to the Balmain ferry, still trying to stifle my sobs. Sitting on the outside deck of the ferry for the short trip along the harbor, chin cupped in my hands, I watched the foaming wake churning in rhythm with my stomach and wondered how I would tell my mother that Mr. Bell now refused to teach me.

"What do you mean Mr. Bell refuses to teach you?" my mother cried in astonishment. "You go back there and get your lesson!"

At that moment, her command was stronger than his, so I lugged my cello all the way back to the Conservatorium only to be rejected again.

The traumatic and humiliating yo-yo process of travelling back and forth to the Conservatorium and having to face the rejection of Mr. Bell, and then home to the stubborn determination of my mother went on for several days, until I finally burst into tears in Gladdy's studio.

"I can't go home until you promise to teach me again. I'll get into trouble" I hiccupped. "I'll get into a lot of trouble."

Poor Gladdy was sufficiently beaten down to accept me again as his student, and for the second time, we started at square one learning how to hold the cello and bow in the traditional fashion. My repertoire eventually expanded – but never again did it include "Faith of our Fathers".

DAD

J ohn O'Carroll was born in Carrick-on-Suir in County Tipperary, Ireland in 1896, the youngest of four children in a family that was plagued by tragedy. His mother died in childbirth, and his father, shortly after, "grieved to death". A baby sister had previously died after being dropped by a nursemaid.

His family had owned several butcher shops in the county and had lived in middle class comfort, but when the parents died, the four orphans – my father, his brother and two sisters – were separated with Dad being bundled off alone to an orphanage in England. He was six years old.

It had been arranged that his two sisters, Margaret and Elly, were to be sent to work as mother's helpers on a sheep station in Outback Australia. Before sailing from England, they were allowed to visit their little brother at the orphanage and with the lack of judgment and the misplaced kindness of young girls, promised their six year-old brother that they would "come back tomorrow".

For a long time, my father asked the nuns at the orphanage each day – "Is it tomorrow yet?"

John eventually returned to Ireland, still a schoolboy, to live with distant cousins and complete his education.

Though the details are not known, the sisters were apparently very badly treated in Australia and Elly finally managed to arrange their passage back to Ireland.

They then took very different paths in their lives. Margaret entered a convent to become a Carmelite nun, and Elly went to London to "go on the stage". She married an army officer who, with his four brothers, died in the trenches of France in the Great War and she was left with a baby son, Cyril, who at the age of twelve died of leukemia. Despite the devastating tragedies she had experienced, Elly remained a woman of strong spirit and optimism. She settled in Chelsea, had a career in the theater and lived a colorful life.

The eldest orphan, twelve year-old James, was placed in a seminary and became a Salesian priest. He was a tiny leprechaun of a man with a slender, poetic face, and eloquent, commanding speech. His consummate love for Ireland and her history became channeled into a mission to further the Irish Cause and to make known the wrongs perpetrated against her people. He too lived in England, and taught history in a British boys' school.

* * *

John O'Carroll was a short man, but he always projected a cocky confidence that made him seem taller. With typical Irish coloring – ruddy skin, clear blue eyes under bushy eyebrows, red hair that browned with maturity – he had a cheeky grin that emphasized the deep cleft in his chin. He enjoyed appearing smartly dressed, and for a reunion photograph taken outside Dublin's Mountjoy Gaol – with thirty-four other former political prisoners, all of whom were dressed very soberly – he posed in a bow tie, wing collar, and, surrounded by somber faces, was the only one smiling.

John O'Carroll in back row third from right.

As my father grew up without the support of parents or any immediate family, he had to depend greatly on his own instincts and judgment. Such a background made the man I knew as a child – a man who filled any room with his presence, maintained a spirit of optimism, and had, as my mother would say, a finger in every pie. Indeed he did. He ran his business, he ran his household, and he ran his children's lives. He energetically involved himself in politics and the Catholic Church, and endless schemes, most of which were meant to lead to that elusive "pot of gold". He chose the name of a lottery ticket with such expectancy and a sense of excitement that we all just knew that this had to be the winning one. And when the lottery ticket was drawn and his hopes dashed, "Well then, the next big win was only around the corner." But of course, his "big win" was in the family he raised and nurtured.

Being a product of the Victorian era, my father was a strict parent, though very devoted to his family. He organized us in a quasi-military fashion, some of which might have been necessary but much of it was a show of bravura. Adamant that to sleep beyond 6am represented absolute laziness, he made sure that none of us sunk into this intolerable condition by cranking up the gramophone, and in later years, a more powerful phonogram, early in the morning and blasting us, and often the neighbors, with rousing marches. "Colonel Bogie" and "The Road to Mandalay" became all too familiar to us at an early age. Tramping through the house and banging on doors, he'd call out in a booming voice "Everybody up. No slothful creatures in MY house!"

Dad had an unusual involvement in home life and seemed to actually enjoy domestic activities, and the authority he could assume in organizing the household. My mother had little interest in his regimented style of domesticity, and she always had more tasks than hands, so on occasions that he decided to "run the household", there was no conflict with her and no domain broached.

He frequently cooked meals, which were then served by him standing at the head of the table, ladle in hand, dishing out from a large pot, one of his culinary concoctions. Often his heavy-handed serving technique would upset my mother. While he called out "Next!", he'd whack the side of the plate with the metal ladle, and was even known to remove slivers of enamel from the dish.

His domestic talents also extended to "interior decorating". He was firm in his conviction that rooms should be painted in high gloss enamel "to wash easily" and in two tones – the upper half of the wall in cream, and the lower half in dark brown or dark green "to hide the dirt". Sometimes, the dividing line was masked with a strip of stenciled paper. Our living room was always wall-papered, usually in a cream-colored pattern. But once, as a surprise for my mother, Dad had the living room walls covered with the most fantastic paper. It was black, with a "tree of life" design of gold and silver leaves, red Chippendale-style flowers, and birds of deep green and blue. I thought it was fabulous! My mother, after the initial shock, sat and wept for a long time.

When not decorating, Dad turned his attention to other matters in the house and often organized grandiose cleaning sprees. On one occasion, we clumsily moved every bed, every chair and every dresser into the small backyard, with my father directing the labor, each wall in the now empty house was roughly washed down. After the application of a thick layer of paste wax, the floors were then polished by us to a high sheen. This was the one part of the cleaning process we enjoyed as it involved seating one of our little brothers on a large burlap bag and methodically dragging him back and forth across the boards, first slowly, and as the floor became more polished, gleefully, faster and faster.

Less entertaining were Dad's "kitchen clean-outs" when he would decide that "every pot in the house needs polishing". He would arm us with copper wire scrubbers and a bucket of sand with the intention of having us assiduously polish up all the cooking vessels. The reality was that nasty green-blue copper marks stained our skin and we whined from the boredom of it all.

We eventually developed an instinct for sensing when these preposterous forays were to occur, and as we grew older and smarter, would declare a need to practice our instruments, sometimes for hours, or at least until the spree was completed or forgotten. Practicing was the one activity that was never interrupted by my parents and so it provided the ideal escape from my father's onerous task-making.

The living room was in constant use for practicing, but often on Sunday nights, Dad would assemble us there for a musical soiree. With my father at the piano, the older children played their instruments and those not as advanced, were encouraged to sing, and often my mother, in a high clear voice, would join in.

Dad loved to recite poetry on these evenings

and inspirited competition among us, once by offering a pound note to the first child who could recite by memory all thirty-four verses of "Gray's Elegy In A Country Church Yard".

My father took great pride in our musical abilities and utilized them in his political pursuits. Long before the use of background music became common, for his election campaigns he had his children play incidental music to accompany some of his public appearances and his radio speeches.

Eileen playing harp and Emmett and Cathleen, violin.

Though he had an alliance with the Labor Party, he ran for office as an Independent, twice for State Parliament and once for the Senate. He pursued political office single-handedly and so was always handicapped by a lack of funds, and although he never won an election, he always had sufficient votes not to lose the deposit that a candidate paid to have his name placed on the ballot.

He often "soap-boxed" in the Domain, an expansive park area in Sydney where it was popular on Sundays for political candidates to voice opinions and causes, and in the days before speaker systems were common, the crowd of listeners would be as large as the speech was interesting. Touched with blarney, Dad spoke with a strong voice and always attracted a large crowd.

During the Thirties, large families were encouraged in Australia as the country had insufficient population for its economic growth. Accompanying my father to the Domain was often our Sunday outing and at some point in his speeches, he would gesture to us, "Come on up here with me, children. Let us show these people what I have done for the country."

Much to our embarrassment, we would have to join him on the platform. On one occasion, when we were being squashed together on the small podium and while my father was boasting "Look at my contribution to Australia. Here are my MY little steps and stairs", this particular little step lost her balance, and went tumbling down the stairs into the crowd, much to the annoyance of my father but to the delight of my brothers and sisters, who relished the dramatic distraction.

There was also a sentimental side to my blustery, quixotic father. Up to the time of his death in 1956, he corresponded constantly with both of his sisters, and his brother James, although he hadn't seen them in more than thirty years. He corresponded too with a Trappist monk in Canada, sometimes enclosing money for prayers for a "special intention". He also regularly purchased a money order to send a donation to Boys Town in Nebraska, U.S.A., undoubtedly remembering the trials of being raised as an orphan himself. To my knowledge he didn't send money to the orphanage in England that was his home for many years, but then I remember his speaking of his life there only once. And the memory is vivid, not because of the story he told, but the manner in which it was interrupted. Until then I hadn't known that men too, could weep.

MADAME LLARRACO

At one end of our kitchen, a black cast-iron fuel stove was set into the fireplace under the open chimney. Always on the warm stove was a kettle of water ready for tea making and in winter, on the back hob, a pot of soup stock was usually simmering. Built-in wooden cupboards surrounded the stove area and unlike the clutter that was typical of most other cupboards in our house, the contents of these were orderly and easily accessible. We knew this because while my parents had always made it clear that we were not to investigate these cupboards as they contained important articles and papers, we were often guilty of succumbing to our childhood curiosity and when left alone, carefully lifting out various items and examining them.

Among these items, two of the possessions that belonged to my mother fascinated me. One was a large brown leather handbag, very worn, and stored inside of it were small bundles of papers tied together with lengths of faded blue ribbon. These held no interest for me so I respected their privacy. But the metal-framed handbag had as its clasp, two very large and smooth amber-colored glass knobs. I enjoyed repeatedly rolling them against each other to open and close the bag thus producing a resonant click that was very satisfying.

On the same shelf, was a large black Gladstone bag that presented a greater challenge to open. I was not successful in figuring out how to work this metal spring lock until my older sister Pat volunteered to demonstrate the operation of this mechanism. The click wasn't as satisfying, but the contents of the bag certainly were. Folded at the top were a number of brightly colored scarves of a very soft and filmy material, and underneath them were two long skirts in vivid shades of orange and pink, the hemlines decorated with dangling gold tassels. We excitedly pulled these out, and for a moment, held the romantic garments up against our waists.

At the bottom of this treasure bag, we found a small silver container, shaped like a purse, and next to it, a pretty tin box stenciled with a pattern of red roses. We opened the tin and inside were several packs of cards. This find was startling as card-playing was forbidden by our parents, though they never offered any reason or explanation (which was true for many of their restrictions). Two of the packs were regular playing cards but the others were unlike anything we had ever seen. The cards didn't have numbers and the usual symbols of spades and hearts on them, but fantastic pictures of exotic women and knights and strange markings. This bag was the most wonderful discovery we had ever made!

The next time Pat and I were left undisturbed in the house, we again lifted down the Gladstone bag and this time, being a little bolder, we each pulled on a long skirt and draped the silky scarves around our necks. Gathering up our hems with one hand, we twirled around and around, exchanging giggling compliments. Giddy from our spinning, we fell to the floor laughing. After regaining our breath, we spread the strange cards across the linoleum to compare the elaborate pictures and admire the unusual illustrations, but could derive no meaning from them.

We then turned our attention to the silver purse and, in the process of examining it, pressed a small button on the side. It instantly popped open, spilling out small white cards, and as we hurriedly picked them up, we could see that each one had inscribed on it in fine script, "MADAME LLARRACO" and under this odd-sounding name, was our phone number – "W1556".

A few evenings later, my father was supervising us at dinner while my mother attended to the baby. Then while we were still eating, she settled her youngest in his crib, put on her coat and hat, lifted the Gladstone bag from the cupboard and saying "Now help your father, won't you", she gave us each her customary kiss on the cheek and left the house.

Pat and I exchanged curious looks across the table. After dinner, in the privacy of our room, we sat on the bed and she whispered to me "I worked it out." Then pulling one of the small white cards from the pocket of her school uniform, she pointed to the strange name, "Look at this! Llarraco is O'Carroll spelt backwards. Madame Llarraco is our Mum!"

This incredible discovery made us look at our mother in a new light; she was no longer just Mum. She was now a much more intriguing person to us and we became very observant of any sign that would offer a clue to solving the Madame Llarraco Mystery. We kept a lookout for when Mum would go to the fireplace cupboards, we would note at what times she would leave the house carrying the bag, and were not above skulking in the doorway when she was talking on the telephone.

The mystery shrouding our mother became all the more compelling to two young sticky beaks when sometimes she would return home from her excursions carrying not only the Gladstone bag, but more importantly, a shopping bag full of delicious treats. Often these were iced cakes or little savories – meat tarts and asparagus rolls – and once she even produced a small box full of silver and white sugared almonds. We were allowed only a few, with the rest put away for a "special occasion".

We were unable to directly ask Mother to reveal her secrets to us. Reflecting the suspicion bred into Irish people by generations of repression, my parents had always instructed us to "never tell anyone your business and never ask anyone theirs." So a clear understanding was established in our household that we were not to ask our mother and father about their activities if they hadn't volunteered the information.

* * *

Further up Darling Street, opposite the park and set in a terrace of small shops, was a tattoo parlor. While it was one of the many places we were instructed to avoid because it attracted "rough types", this directive never stopped me from walking past it and gazing in the window with fascination. Displayed on the walls were the many examples and designs that for a few shillings, could become permanent artwork on an adventurous man's chest or arms. And sometimes when it was very hot, the tattoo artist, shirtless and dripping with perspiration, would sit on a high stool in the doorway with his pots of ink and fine needles, meticulously decorating a weathered seaman.

Besides the examples of tattoo designs, the

parlor window often held odd items marked with a sale price. It usually included a few pieces of ladies jewelry or a man's watch, and once, on display was a large, slightly used box of Windsor & Newton water-color paints complete with a ceramic palette, a collection of various-sized paint brushes, and tubes and tubes of every imaginable color begging to be squeezed. I instantly knew that owning this box of paints would make my life complete. Gathering my courage, I entered the fantastical parlor and shyly asked the tattoo artist the price of it. "Just for you, love – if you buy it today – I'll make a special price of ten shillings."

I quickly ran home, knowing my parents would be thrilled that I wanted to be an artist. Secure in the knowledge that they wouldn't pass up such a bargain, I asked them for the money for this wonderful box of paints explaining that the tattoo man was giving me a special price just for today. My mother again failed to recognize my potential for greatness, and instead of showing pride in her daughter's ambitions, expressed only anger at her disobedience.

"You've been told to never go near that tattoo parlor. What were you even doing on that side of the street! Are you thick or something?" My ability to become a painter wasn't even acknowledged. "Ten shillings indeed! Do you think money grows on trees?"

After the incident with the box of paints, I refrained from sharing my knowledge of the changes of display in the tattoo parlor window, and one day as I was passing, I came to a dead halt, arrested by the sight of a spread of picture cards exactly the same as those we had discovered in my mother's Gladstone bag. The artist was leaning against the doorway smoking a cigarette.

"I see you've got your eye on those Tarot Cards. Will I show them to you?" he offered.

Reaching into the window, he gestured me into the shop and spread the picture cards out on the glass countertop. Standing on tip-toe, I watched and listened, completely absorbed, as the artist held up to advantage, a card showing a barefoot woman dressed in a tunic, holding a crescent moon, and then one of a dark-cloaked man on a horse. He explained the meanings of some of these mysterious figures and how the Tarot Cards were used for fortune-telling.

This time, I made my way home slowly, taking care to cross to our side of Darling Street as soon as I had left the parlor, contemplating this new, crucial information.

I looked for Pat and proudly told her "Guess what? I found out something. Those strange picture cards in Mum's bag are for telling fortunes."

"How would you know?" Pat queried me with skepticism.

"The tattoo man told me." My source removed any of her doubt.

We then shared our thoughts on all that we now knew and finally reached the conclusion that our mother, Madame Llarraco, was dressing like a gypsy and going off and telling fortunes. On one hand, we were a little excited by the glamour of this occupation but also resented the fact that she led this other secret life that excluded us.

We approached Cathleen with our information and complaints, feeling a little smug that for once we knew something that our older sister didn't, but also hoping for the wisdom of a third party.

She didn't look surprised at all but eyed us accusingly, "You little sneaks. I have a good mind to tell on you." My sister continued to chide us, "You've been going through Mum's bag, haven't you? What business is that of yours, you selfish pair of troublemakers. You should think about Mum for a change."

This remark seemed unfair. We had thought of little else lately.

"Anyhow, I already know about everything you've told me" boasted Cathleen. "As a matter of fact, she took me along last week to a fortune-telling job. It was fun. We went into the city on the tram and then caught a bus to a lovely house in Rose Bay. There were lots of ladies there having a special afternoon tea, and they gave me some too."

We listened to our older sister, surprised and envious. "A booth was set up right in the living room and the ladies took turns to go in and have their fortunes told my Mum." Cathleen continued to regale us with her adventure, "After she came out of the booth, Mum had some afternoon tea too and then read some of the ladies' tea cups and before we left, one lady gave Mum a box of cakes and said to take it home to the other children. Don't you remember those pink cakes we had last week?"

❋ ❋ ❋

My mother had learned fortune-telling in Ireland as a girl from her grandmother, who was well-known for her ability to read the future. Recognizing a psychic gift in her granddaughter, she taught her to read not only Tarot cards and palms, but also interpret fortunes from tea leaves, the tracings of beer foam on a glass and the markings left on a dish from a swirled, beaten egg white.

Coping with the difficulties of raising a family during the Depression, my mother used her fortune-telling skills to supplement our income, accepting engagements at private homes and functions. She had a large clientele and was popular and respected. In addition, quite often a well-dressed stranger, always a woman, would enter our shop asking for Mother, and after a short whispered conference, Mum would escort her through the back of the shop into the living room with firm instructions to us that she was not to be disturbed. These clients, wanting anonymity and a more in-depth reading than they could comfortably request at a public function, would travel across town to a suburb where they were unknown to seek my mother's advice.

Mother took her gifts seriously and didn't attempt to pass any of her skills on to us, maintaining with her fortune-telling, a very private and separate life. Consequently, she didn't engage in Tarot Card reading with her children, but occasionally read our tea leaves. Sometimes at the dinner table, she thoughtfully picked up one of our tea cups, gently rotating it and silently examining the configuration of leaves. This gesture usually elicited cries, "Oh Mum, please tell us what you see in the tea leaves!"

The cup was just as likely to be returned wordlessly to its saucer, but at times, she voiced her thoughts to us, her captivated audience.

DANNY BOY

My parents were very active in the Irish community in Sydney and much of their social and cultural support came from within this group, but they also had a wide circle of friends and acquaintances of different nationalities. As a child I was often teased or taunted because I didn't have "good Aussie English", but had speech that was colored with an Irish brogue. And in turn, I often had difficulty in understanding the accented speech of some of my parents' visitors.

A favorite occasional outing for us was the long train ride to an outlying suburb to visit a German family, the Butters. They had a large yard with laden orange trees, many varieties of vegetables growing and a nanny-goat of which I was very afraid. Once Mr. Butter took the time to show me the difference between a small pullet egg, and a regular hen's egg. Then he amazed me with a large duck egg and finally, eyes twinkling, produced an enormous grey-green sphere and I could only understand two words of his guttural speech – "gross" and "emu".

I was at a class at the Conservatorium one day when a young student was rewarded with approving laughter, when, referring to one of our new music professors, he curved his index finger over his nose, saying "me no speak da English". I didn't understand the gesture, but noting the mirth his remark created, repeated it when I got home. The back of my father's hand sent me reeling and while no explanation was offered, it was clear to me that this gesture and remark were unacceptable.

* * *

My mother had a very good friend, Danny Goldblum, who owned a pawn shop at the top of Oxford Street. In her aggravating Irish way, she only ever called him Danny Boy. Among other goods offered in his shop, Danny received consignments of clothing form society women and he always set aside evening dresses or costumes that he thought would be useful for our family members for concert performances or indeed, suitable items for Madame Llarraco. He knew the history of each gown, so could be relied upon to prevent the embarrassment that could occur if the same dress appeared first on a hostess, but later on a performer. When he received an interesting shipment, he would write a brief note to my mother to inform her. Many times I was allowed to accompany Mum to Danny Boy's shop, first taking the tram to the city and then two more trams to reach the square at the top of Oxford Street. We always brought along an empty suitcase and some string bags.

Danny Boy would warmly greet Mum at his doorway – "It's May! How are you my dear?"

She would sit in his office and gossip and drink tea with him while I was allowed to explore his dark, musty shop, which was a treasure trove to a curious child. The glass cases displayed racks of watches, rings, bundles of spoons and numbers of personal souvenir items such as trophies and engraved trays, which were mute testimony to their owners' previous glories. The shelves held suitcases, trunks, small radios and occasionally a banjo or trumpet. Men's suits were draped over chairs and in a deep sink in the corner were piled dirty teacups and ashtrays.

After an hour or so of sorting through clothing, we would leave the shop with our suitcase crammed with some of Danny Boy's selections and then walk down the crowded footpath of Oxford Street, occasionally stopping to purchase fruit and vegetables from the bargain barrows that appeared on each block. By the time we arrived home we were weary and the string bags were heavy and expanded to capacity.

Not only did Danny Boy provide Mother with inexpensive costumes and dresses, but also the occasional client for her fortune telling jobs. In turn, European migrants, referred to my mother by Danny, frequently came into our barber shop.

These men, who often suffered the indignity of being called "Reffo's" – a common Australian term for refugees – would greet Mum with a lift of their hat. They would open on the counter a battered Globite school case displaying their goods, which were usually cards of needles and pins, as well as aprons and potholders made by their wives. Mother was always sympathetic, understanding how difficult their lives were. She would offer a simple meal and a few words of advice to these men, who had very limited English, but supported their families by walking miles each day selling goods from a suitcase.

Once I told Mum that I needed a gift for a teacher and she took me upstairs to her bedroom and opened the bottom drawer of her dressing table. I was astonished to see that it was crammed with dozens of homemade aprons and potholders and a lifetime supply of needles and pins.

TARA HARP ENSEMBLE

Eileen's harp stood in the corner of the living room, near the doorway, shrouded in a fitted cover of heavy bronze wool with ties of black grosgrain binding. When she prepared to practice or rehearse with my brother, Eileen deftly lifted her harp from the corner and placed it in the center of the room. With the quick practiced movements, she unlaced the black ties and lifted the heavy cover from the gold-columned instrument, and rolling it up, laid it on the floor near the staircase. Then returning her attention to the harp, she tuned it, her head turned to the side in concentration as she rotated the pin with a large metal tuning key held in her right hand, and plucked the strings with her left hand, testing the octaves and fifths.

For a little girl, to watch this ballet of preparation by my older sister, the prelude to the presentation of the resplendent harp, the movement of it to center stage, and the finale where Eileen ran her thumb and forefinger up and down the strings in glissando as a final test of the tuning, was absorbing and completely glamorous.

In their teenage years, Eileen and Emmett

helped support the family by performing music at social functions and their rehearsals at home were most often at night when the small children were in bed and the living room could offer necessary quiet. At these times, if I was still awake, I would leave my bed and sit in the dark at the top of the stairs, listening to the music and the buzzing sounds of discussion. Then every few moments, I would slide down one more stair until finally I sat on the bottom step and was able to see into the illuminated living room and watch my sister seated at her harp, the light shining on her long titian hair, and my brother standing confidently as he swept his bow over his violin. Often my parents were seated on the couch, enjoying this time of rare leisure and the chance to hear their two oldest children make music.

If I was unobserved to this point, it was then a small matter to reach over to the bronze wool harp cover folded on the floor near me, and silently creep under it, nestling in the warm darkness of this cozy hideaway. The goal of successfully hiding under the cover kept me alert and cautious up to this point, but once enfolded by it, I relaxed and heard little more of the voices and music.

I would be awakened by the sudden light as the cover was removed from me and by the sound of my father's voice, as he lifted me from under the bronze folds, saying gently, "Look what I found this time. Isn't this a surprise" and half asleep, I would be carried back up to my bed.

* * *

When my sister and brother worked together as a duo, they rehearsed at home, but they also extended to form a large group and its size varied according to the requirements of the engagement. The publicity flyer for the group read:

> *The Tara Harp Ensemble is open for all engagements whether public or private, large or small, Weddings, Banquets, At Homes, etc. The ensemble may be engaged in part, to suit the requirements of the host or hostess: Solos, Duets, Trios or Quartettes. The full combination consists of two harps, two violins, viola and cello, piano as desired.*

The manager was one "Lewis Quann".

Catering to the musical tastes of their audience, the Tara Harp Ensemble would perform popular music of the time and were often engaged to play at "Sydney's leading social rendezvous, Elizabeth Bay House" and also the various embassies in Sydney.

When the full ensemble performed, they wore a splendid matching set of costumes, undoubtedly supplied by Danny Boy. The women were attired in colorful gathered skirts decorated with bands

74

of satin ribbon, and velvet bodices laced down the front over peasant-style blouses. A tiara-style headpiece of colored satin with streamers of ribbons flowing from either side completed the outfit. Usually my brother was the lone male performer. He was a handsome sight in a loose, white satin shirt with flowing sleeves, black trousers and a wide red satin sash. On his head he wore a Tyrolean-style hat of green felt with a feather on the side. Occasionally, Cathleen, although only seven years old, was also pressed into service, and in this Shirley Temple era, charmed the audience with her precocious playing, wearing a shortened version of the costume with patent leather shoes, and sporting a head full of bouncing curls.

Transporting the harp and music stands to the different venues presented a challenge for the ensemble that was well met by their versatile manager, Lewis Quann, a.k.a. John O'Carroll. My father would borrow from our local greengrocer, Mr. Whalen, a flatbed truck, tie down the instruments and stands securely on the back, and exercising ingenious economy, squeeze Eileen and Emmett in the front of the truck with him. He would drive to within a few blocks of the venue, dropping them off at a taxi stand where they then hired a cab to drive them to the front door in dignified splendor.

Dad subsequently donned a dust coat and cap and drove to the service entry and assuming the role, not of manager Lewis Quann, but of the Ensemble's delivery man, carried in the harp and set up music stands and chairs, so that the stage was set for the elegant entrance of the Tara Harp Ensemble.

Following the evening's performance, Eileen and Emmett, after receiving congratulations and payment from the host, caught a cab home. My father returned to the hall and again tied down the harp, stands, and boxes of music on the truck platform, finally arriving back at our house much later than my sister and brother.

Sometimes I heard the cab pull up when Eileen and Emmett arrived home. From the top of the staircase, I would look down in wonder at this glamorous couple in evening clothes as they came into the house, often carrying a gift presented to them, a bouquet of flowers or a beribboned box of chocolates, and flushed with the success of their performance.

I resolved at a very young age that when I grew up, I too would earn my living by appearing on the stage in a beautiful long gown, playing music, and I would always come home in a taxi cab.

BATHROOM PUNISHMENT

Our home, like most houses built in the mid-nineteenth century, had at the back of the yard an outhouse, known in Australia as the "Dunny". The very narrow lane that ran between the houses was called the "Dunny Lane". In the years before sewage was installed, one indispensable council worker was the "Dunny man". Wearing brief shorts and a sturdy leather yoke to protect his shoulders, he would run down these lanes in the early morning, collect each filled Dunny can, and with great skill, hoist it onto his shoulder, run back, and secure it on the Dunny cart to be hauled away.

So, unlike modern homes, the toilet was a completely separate facility to the bathroom, which in our house was an iron-roofed timber shed adjoining the kitchen, with a backyard entrance. It had a claw foot bathtub and a sink with a tap underneath for the garden hose, which was stored coiled up on the grey cement floor. The door had an 18-inch space at the top for ventilation, and on the wall, above a long slatted bench, hung the only mirror in the house.

When I was naughty, which was reasonably

often, my father, as a form of punishment, would confine me in the bathroom. This banishment secretly delighted me as then I had the whole room to myself to dance, mime and act in front of the precious mirror.

It was also the one opportunity I had to transform myself into the person whom I admired and envied most – Shirley Temple. Stuffed at the back of the cupboard next to the bathtub, just for these occasions, I kept a wig which I had made from scraps of sisal rope. After having unwound each piece of rope, I had soaked them in water and then wrapped the strands around old wooden cotton spools, and when they had dried and the spools were removed, each wound piece became a corkscrew curl. I had made dozens of these curls and attached them with bobby-pins to a length of ribbon so that when I tied this band around my head, bow on top, I could quickly change from an ordinary girl with straight brown, bobbed hair to Shirley Temple.

Standing on the bench with the mirror all to myself, I would toss my rope curls back dramatically, then flip them coyly over my face with the back of my hand, and look up to the mirror with raised eyes and pouted lips. Changing moods, I would then assume a beaming smile and crinkle my nose, all the time bobbing my head from side to side to achieve the full effect of bouncing, golden curls. So with the hope that my father would unwittingly punish me with this sought-after privacy in our bathroom, I often misbehaved.

Cathleen fulfilled an unappreciated role as my protective older sister, always feeling sorry for me when I was disciplined in this manner. Too often she would sit outside the bathroom door and pleaded "Oh Daddy, please let her out. She'll be scared in there all alone. Let her out of the bathroom. I'll take care of her."

Needless to say, I resented this interference and would be on the other side of the door prancing and posing in front of the mirror wishing she'd mind her own business and go away. Sometimes her pleading touched my father's heart enough so that he would say "Alright then, you look after her."

Hearing this remark and before he could unlatch the door, I would have to abruptly interrupt my performance, pull off and hide my wig, and quickly sit on the bench, with my head in my hands, looking contrite.

One summer day when the temperature soared to the century mark, I made sure that my behavior warranted incarceration as the bathroom was the coolest place in the house. I had just put some cold water in the bathtub, and sitting on the edge, was enjoying splashing my bare feet about when once again, Cathleen sat outside the door and started wailing – "Please let her out, she'll be good, she'll be good. I'll look after her."

This time I was fed up with my sister and decided that no longer was I going to have her rain on my parade. I stepped out of the bathtub, crept over to the garden hose and stealthily uncoiled it. Carefully placing the nozzle just over the top of the door, I tip-toed over to the tap and quickly turned it on full blast. I was rewarded with a startled shriek! Not only did my sister's pleading cease, but my father then shouted over the door "Alright, just for that, you can stay in there longer!"

CATHOLIC VS. PUBLIC SCHOOL

As the enrollment of young O'Carrolls at St. Augustine's increased, so did an appreciation for them by the teachers. They were good students and also brought the added dimension of musical talent to this local Catholic school. My father too, was aware of our value as a collective asset to the school community which he was not above using when it suited him.

Top L-R: Sean, Maureen, Cathleen, Patricia & Seamus
Bottom L-R: Eileen, Liam, John, May, Eamon & Emmett

The local Irish priest often visited our home socially in the evening and he would sit at the kitchen table with a cup of tea and share remembrances of Ireland with my mother. But as the evening wore on and Mother retired, he then became involved in discussions, and sometimes disagreements with my father, and on occasion there came the sound of raised-voices and fists pounding on the kitchen table punctuating impassioned arguments over world problems and politics. Who had won the latest political debate sometimes became apparent the next morning when my father, at the breakfast table, would darkly state "You're all going to the Public school today."

It didn't help to protest - "But I did my homework for Sister Teresa."

"Don't answer back, you're going to the Public school."

Having the Catholic and Public schools directly opposite each other with only a narrow street as a buffer, gave students the opportunity to exploit the religious and cultural animosity between them, and despite the teachers' attempts at maintaining neutrality, a lot of name calling occurred at recess. Typical was a Public leaning over the fence and yelling "Protestants, Protestants, ring the bell. Catholics, Catholics, go to hell."

So to enter a Public school even temporarily as a Catholic, and worse, as an Irish Catholic, was to enter the Lion's den. I don't know what arrangement my father made with the Public school teachers but fortunately they, unlike the students, appeared to accept the occasional sudden appearance of O'Carrolls with good grace.

There were exceptions though. Our household was pro-Irish and with this came the inevitable anti-British attitude which presented more of a problem for the teachers at the Public school than for the nuns at St. Augustine's. This sentiment was implicit even in our music-making at home where on many evenings, with my father playing an accompaniment, we gathered around the piano and sang songs. At the time, I didn't fully realize that most of these were Irish revolutionary songs.

Sometimes when heavy rain precluded outdoor sport activities, a teacher would instead organize an ad hoc talent show. Each student took their turn. One girl would give her clumsy rendition of a tap dance while another, with dramatic arm gestures, would stumble thought a chestnut like "The Boy Stood on the Burning Deck". Once, one bold student draped herself in the ever-present Union Jack and after singing "Rule Brittania" was rewarded with enthusiastic applause and cheers from the class. When my turn came, having noted that a song got the best reception and anticipating a similar response, I was utterly bewildered when the teacher rudely interrupted my fervent singing of "They're Hanging Kevin Barry" with –

"Sit down, O'Carroll! We'll have none of that Irish trouble-making in my classroom."

Empire Day at the Public school presented more problems. This was an important holiday all over Australia which honored the foundation of the British Empire with speeches, tableaux, flag waving, and prominent displays of the portraits of the King and the Royal Family. We were not sent to school but always kept home on this day, away from any celebrations which honored the British Empire.

The following day, the teacher would question me – "Why were you absent yesterday?"

"I was home sick."

"How interesting. Your brothers and sisters were absent too. Were they also sick?"

"Yes, my father says we always get sick on Empire Day."

Needless to say, it must have been a relief to the teachers of the Public school when my father and the priest eventually settled their differences and we were again shuffled back to St. Augustine's. The capricious notice to return to the Fold was always as brief as his order had been to leave St. Augustine's and was often nothing more than a simple statement at breakfast – "I've decided that you can go back to St. Augustine's today."

THE PUBLIC HEALTH DENTIST

There was an occasion when I returned to the Public school from St. Augustine's with particular unwillingness – for a visit to the public health dentist. While his temporary surgery was set up in the Public school, he examined and treated all students, including us Papists. The thought of this visit made us very nervous and I asked my mother if I really needed to go. Rightfully suspicious of the treatment offered, she replied "No, you don't have to go to any public health dentist."

The week of his visit, Mother Clement came into our classroom, calling out the names of the next relay of students to be sent over to the Public school, but when she reached my desk I confidently told her that my mother said I didn't have to go to any public health dentist. Mother Clement didn't even favor me with a glance but repeated my name in a louder voice, and I too was marched across the street with the other unfortunates. We fearfully sat outside the surgery, looking at each other with doubt every time another wail was heard from behind the closed door. Then a tear-stricken girl emerged holding a cloth to her bloodied mouth, validating our terror.

By the time my name was called, my mind was racing as to how I could escape this chamber of horrors. I was seated in a chair next to a tray of gruesome-looking instruments and the dentist, assisted by a large, fierce-looking nurse, commanded me to open my mouth. I gagged while he poked around my teeth with a sharp metal probe and when he reached to the tray of instruments for what appeared to be a pair of pincers, and said - "I think some of these baby teeth can come out" - my escape plans hatched.

As he leant over me, I quickly drew up my knees, thrusting my feet against his chest. He fell back against his nurse, knocking over the tray of instruments, and I took the opportunity to bolt from the chair and run back to school. I sat at my desk, naively confident that the ordeal was over, and calmly resumed work.

It wasn't quite that easy. Bad news travels fast and in a short while Mother Clement swished into the classroom and with a shocked look on her face, demanded "Would the Agent of the Devil please stand up?"

I knew she meant me but nonetheless glanced around hopefully, then lowered my head trying to remain inconspicuous. I became aware of a dark shadow cast over my desk and looked up again, into the angry face of Mother Clement. Her hand shot out from beneath her habit and I was yanked to my feet.

"Maureen O'Carroll has disgraced our school!" she announced to the class.

Mother Clement poked a stiff finger into my back all the way to St. Augustine's church and made me kneel in front of the crucifix by the entrance say an act of contrition. Then pointing to the wounds of Christ, she demanded "Would Our Lord have done such a thing? Did Christ kick his tormentors?"

I could only think that Christ too was bloodied by his tormentors, so passivity did not pay, and maybe he should have kicked them and run! But in the darkened church, with the Mother Superior inculcating in me the example of the crucified Christ, my sense of self-protection became overwhelmed by a desire for martyrdom.

Now prepared to face my fate, I returned to the dentist, who pushed me into the chair – "You're the nasty little girl who kicked me. I have something special for nasty little girls like you."

A spatula of brown powder was pressed on my tongue. It tasted horrible and stung badly.

My nemesis then said "You are not going to be bad anymore, are you?"

All thought of being a Christian martyr disappeared and again I had to plot an escape – "Oh no, I won't be bad and I'm truly sorry."

"That's more like it."

Resuming his dental duties, he again reached for the set of pincers. As he approached me with this weapon, my instincts took over and in a replay of earlier events, I thrust my feet against his chest, and again he fell back against the tray of instruments. But this time I had more sense than to return to the classroom and instead, ran all the way home. Fortunately my mother didn't question my early arrival and I was more than pleased to be particularly helpful to her.

At St. Augustine's the next day, I received a tongue lashing again about disgracing the school but I was blissfully unconcerned. I still had my baby teeth.

Maureen O'Carroll

THE ANCHOR
HAIRDRESSING SALON

2 20 Darling Street was a free-standing, two-storey terrace house in which we lived and many of us had been born.

The centre of activity was the kitchen which was furnished with a wood-burning stove, a sink, hanging mesh food keepers and a large rectangular wooden table with benches on either side where we had all of our meals, where homework was done and, when padded with an old blanket, doubled as an ironing board. Also on the first floor was the living room which despite the lack of space in the house, my parents managed to maintain as a parlor. It was dominated by a large stuffed couch and matching armchair upholstered in brown velvet. These were not to be sat upon by us and neither were we permitted to play in this room, but as it housed the piano, harps and other instruments, we were allowed to practice there. The walls were covered in heavy textured cream and brown paper popular at the time, and hung at regular intervals, in ornate gilded frames, were portraits of Irish heroes.

The cedar staircase from the living room led to three upstairs bedrooms. My parents had the largest of these at the front of the house while the other two were fitted out with bunk beds accommodating the girls in one and the boys in the other.

The living room had another doorway which led through to our barber shop, the Anchor Hairdressing Salon. If the kitchen was the hub of activity for our family, the Anchor was certainly a hub of activity for much of Balmain.

Facing Darling Street, the main thoroughfare of Balmain, the salon was well situated for business in an area bustling with activity. Within a short distance was the large Colgate-Palmolive soap factory, the Poole & Steel shipworks, three ferry wharves and the London Hotel. Every few minutes, trams clattered by in both directions, with brazen young paper boys jumping on and off the moving cars, crying out in a nasal voice "payp'rr, payp'rr" and dispensing newspapers from the pile held under one arm and with the other, collecting money and making change from a leather pouch strapped around their waist.

While there were very few cars or trucks along Darling Street, noisy street vendors were common, peddling their goods from horse-drawn carts or hand barrows, attracting customers with street cries for their various specialized items and services – "Bottle-O, bottles and rags, Bottle-O", "Clothes poles, clothes poles!" and a cry very popular with the housewives – "Rabbit-O, cooked stuffed rabbits, Rabbit-O!"

Adding to the chorus of calls on Darling Street, was the Anchor's resident hawker, which was in fact a green parrot, stationed outside the salon in a large cage. Dad had trained the popular bird to repeatedly screech "Haircut, Sixpence! Shave, Three pence!"

Inside the salon, there were two chrome and leather barber chairs, each sporting a heavy leather razor strap. Within easy reach was the plate glass countertop which held a number of straight razors, combs, brushes, a small electric towel warmer, as well as jars and bottles of brightly coloured and perfumed products. All of these items were doubled from the reflection of the large mirror on the wall behind the countertop. Unmatched chairs, always occupied by locals, were set about in the salon, close enough for conversation and handy to standing ashtrays weighted with sand.

For a child, sometimes allowed to sit in the doorway and watch the activities, the Anchor was a most fascinating place.

While my quiet Uncle John did most of the barbering, Dad, in his usual theatrical manner, reigned over this salon. When he shaved one of

 the men, he first honed the straight razor on the strap with great flourishes and then tested its sharpness with the ball of his thumb. After vigorously lathering the face with a foam-laden brush, he deftly removed the soapy whiskers with a dramatic series of long strokes. Then wrapping the clean-shaven face in a steaming towel, he patted it with unnecessarily loud claps, and with a magician-like gesture, removed the towel from the reddened face and lastly, applied a splash of aftershave, all the time talking. If the client's hair had also been cut, Dad completed the toilette by dipping a small, soft brush in a basin of talcum powder and with fast, painting-like movements, he brushed the man's neck, sending puffs of perfumed powder into the air.

Besides barbering, Dad also conducted other businesses at the Anchor, including a tobacconist and a gift shop. A large glass showcase beneath the cash register held a variety of small gifts and toiletries. The top shelf displayed men's items including amber cigarette holders, leather tobacco pouches, pipes, lighters, tie pins and belts. The small selection of women's' gifts was typically linen handkerchiefs, small bottles of Eau de Cologne, soaps and trinkets. They served Dad's customers well for last minute dashes to his salon to placate an upset wife on a forgotten wedding anniversary or birthday.

The men's' toiletries offered were mostly manufactured by my father and he catered to the custom of the era, when a man's concession to good grooming was to plaster his hair down with brilliantine and apply a liberal splash of Bay Rum to his cheeks and neck. In an area at the back of the house, Dad heated large tins of Vaseline, adding perfume and an intense red powder, cochineal. The colored liquid was then poured into fancy jars, and when solidified, decorated with green and gold labels embossed with "ANCHOR BILLIANTINE". This was a popular item as was his homemade Bay Rum aftershave, and as a customer felt renewed with a haircut and shave, it was quite easy to also sell him these items to maintain his grooming at home.

The most popular feature of the Anchor, however, was not the barbering, the tobacco items or the gifts, but Dad's other business – his "lending library".

Housed in a partitioned area at the back of the barber shop, was a small collection of books which included volumes of Macaulay's History, The Complete Works of Benjamin Disraeli, and The Novels of Lord Lytton, all undoubtedly purchased as a lot by my father at an auction. They were dry and unreadable Victorian works, but they weren't meant to be read. One of dad's side-lines was bookmaking. He wasn't binding more volumes for the library but taking bets on the horse races. Bookmaking was an illegal activity, but this didn't stop many shopkeepers from engaging in it, and my father enjoyed maintaining a unique system to disguise the betting; a borrowed book would be returned with the bet and money placed inside, and another book would be checked out ready for the next bet.

On Saturdays, the Anchor was a social center for many local men, who were off work that day and would evade their share of household chores by insisting to their wives that they need a haircut or shave. But of course barbering wasn't the main attraction. Saturday was the most important day for horse racing and consequently, a particularly busy one for the lending library. Clutching their Lord Lytton novels, the men would hover around the radio in the smoke-filled Anchor, engrossed by the announcer's incessant monologue of race results from tracks around the country, and as this was thirsty work, they took turns carrying a billy can up the street to the London Hotel to be filled and refilled.

The lending library was enjoying a burgeoning patronage when my father fell victim to an informer. It was suspected that the woman who ran the comic book shop a few doors away didn't appreciate the competition, and one day two policemen came into the Anchor – "We're sorry Jack, but we have to take in your account books." They probably were sorry too, also being patrons of the lending library. My father didn't say anything but looking unconcerned, beamed one of his cheeky grins and proudly handed over his ledgers. All of his records had been written in Gaelic.

Gaelic was not a common written language in Australia and while many Irish people may have spoken the ancient Celtic tongue, there were very few who read it. An attempt was made by the authorities to find a translator. The search was unsuccessful, and even if there was someone who could translate Gaelic, no self-respecting Irish person would have ever agreed to be employed in such a fashion.

Without the required evidence, the case was dropped and my father resumed his concerns at the Anchor, congratulated by all the eager literary members of his lending library.

AGENT OF THE DEVIL

Balmain was an industrial suburb and in many families the children's destiny was to leave school at the legal age and secure a job at the local Palmolive soap factory or the Poole & Steele shipworks. My ambitious parents, who could also be snobs when it suited them, wanted more for us, and from us, even though their income didn't support this. With hopes for their ten children to become professional musicians, they had us spend a lot of our time practicing, going to the Conservatorium, and performing. Leading this different lifestyle meant that we were often isolated by other children at school. Being first generation Australian, we also had a strong brogue so were further isolated by that great assimilator, the Australian accent.

At school, classmates would mock my speech – "Hey O'Carroll, say down town."

Words that sounded like "doone toone" emerged guaranteeing guffaws from my tormentors.

Like all school children, I wanted to be one of the "group" and tried to develop pronunciation techniques that would make me sound just like them. In the privacy of our bathroom, I would stand in front of the mirror and stretch my mouth apart with both hands trying to broaden my vowels by repeating "Dowwwwn, Towwwwn. Dowwwn, Towwwn." It didn't work.

So my accent, along with other social factors, did not enhance my quest for popularity at school. During recess, a favorite game with the girls was to reenact scenes from the movie they had seen at the Hoyts Theater the previous Saturday afternoon. I was seldom allowed the luxury of attending these matinees as my parents considered them a "waste of time and money". So to avoid the embarrassment of admitting that I wasn't part of this Saturday ritual, I would instead ask the teachers for extra assignments to do during recess. This did not sit well with my less-dedicated classmates and I was soon labeled a "teacher's pet".

There was a time however when I lost favor even with the nuns in one of my attempts to ingratiate myself with my schoolmates. Some smirking girls had approached me before class and offered me a shilling if, after our teacher entered the classroom, I would take the first letters of the words, "Father, Uncle, Cousin, King" and put them together and then say the word to the nun. Here was my big chance to be popular... and rich!

Sister Sebastian made her entrance, a hush descended, and a clear confident voice said the magic word, "F**K". She gasped.

"What did you say?" she asked me in a strained whisper.

"F**K"

Worldly as I was, I had not heard this word before but I could see that it was making a strong impression. Even my classmates were speechless. Sister Sebastian gestured to the girl nearest the door "Run and get Mother Clement."

Mother Clement, with fast mincing steps and hands tucked under the bib of her habit, quickly made the short journey from her office, "Sister Sebastian, what is the problem here?"

"Maureen O'Carroll, repeat for Mother what you just said!"

"I said, F**K."

Hands appeared from under her habit and a dervish-like Mother Clement descended on me grabbing my shoulders. "I can't believe one of my girls would say such a thing! Father Murphy will deal with this" she exclaimed.

Like two great black hawks with a baby sparrow between them, the religieuses marched a bewildered girl to the Presbytery.

Father Murphy, in his long dark cassock, was walking up and down on the verandah of the Pres-

bytery saying his Office. He looked up expect-
antly as the trio hurried towards him.

Red-faced with exertion and anger, Mother
Clement sternly demanded "Now Miss, you repeat
to Father Murphy the disgraceful word you said in
Sister Sebastian's classroom."

I knew something was terribly wrong and my
confidence was long gone. This time the F-word
emerged from my trembling lips in a question-
ing whisper. Father Murphy took off his spectacles
and thoughtfully polished them with the corner
of his loose sleeve. A curious wrinkle appeared at
the edges of his mouth and he look at me with
kind eyes. "Maureen, do you know what that word
means?"

"Yes, I think so. It means I get a shilling from the
other girls."

He was silent for a moment then glanced across
to Mother Clement, "I think that Maureen realizes
now that she mustn't use such language. So let's
put this unfortunate incident behind us." Father
Murphy then addressed me, "I want you to go back
to the classroom with the nuns and promise me
you will never say that word again."

The storm in the teacup was over and I was
silently escorted back to class. The girls were sitting there, nervously quiet, but I still had some
unfinished business and turned to them – "Alright,
where's my shilling?"

WAVERLY

In the seaside area of Sydney called Waverly, there is a large, old historic cemetery. Isolated in the Catholic section there, with the blue Pacific as a backdrop, is an impressive white marble memorial, which commemorates Irish resistance to English rule and acknowledges the Irish identity in Australia. In 1898, it was: *erected by the Irish people and sympathizers in Australasia in loving memory of all who dared and suffered for Ireland in 1798.*

On every Easter Sunday of my childhood, we

made a pilgrimage to Waverly as confirmation of my parents' commitment to all that the monument represented, and as an opportunity for their children to become further aware of their heritage.

Easter week became a time when my parents spoke with veneration of the patriots honored by this memorial: the Irish leader, Wolfe Tone, and other heroes of the 1798 rebellion; and the martyrs of the 1916 Easter Uprising, whose names had been later carved into the marble base. The 1916 names had particular significance to my parents as they had known all of these men from their own participation in the Easter revolt and had even named four of their sons after them.

A flurry of activity always occurred in our house on Easter Saturday in preparation for the Sunday service. My father would reverently remove from the wardrobe the tri-colored Irish flag that he had brought from Ireland, and fetch from the florist the pre-ordered large laurel wreath, which was always decorated with green, white and gold satin ribbons. Every year, in an elegant script, he wrote on a gold-edged card to be pinned to the wreath, a motto, such as -

He who dies for liberty, lives forever.

In the chilly pre-dawn hours of Easter Sunday, we were roused from sleep, dressed and bundled into our coats. Gradually, there would be knocks on the door from other participants who lived in the neighborhood and always gathered at our house for the trip.

As each person came in from the cold and was handed a cup of hot tea to warm them, the small living room soon became steamy, crowded, and filled with an air of social excitement. As the adults softly chatted, they pinned on each other's lapels a simple rosette, made by my mother, of three narrow ribbons, also in green, white and gold. Then Mr. Whelan, the greengrocer, would drive his large flatbed truck up to the front door. Mary MacQuaid, the oldest participant, would be seated next to the driver and given the laurel wreath, which she would cradle protectively on her lap. The rest of us crowded onto the back of the truck, standing and balancing together, with the men forming a human perimeter around the women and children, who were positioned in the cramped space in the middle.

My earliest memories of these trips are of the comforting smells of damp wool and smoky tweed while clinging to a trousered or lisle-clad leg in the stifling warmth of the back of the truck as it swayed carefully with its human cargo on the deserted roads to Waverly. Finally, Mr. Whelan would slide to a stop at the cemetery gates, and the more nimble jumped off the truck and helped the women and older men down. Those of us who were small children were greeted with a rush of cold fresh air as we were hoisted up and then placed on the ground, our legs still wobbling from having balanced so long on the moving truck. Slowly, we all filed down the hill to the memorial, its imposing Celtic cross silhouetted against the pale morning sky, and we congregated on the grassy strip in front of the monument as the dawn heralded Easter Sunday.

Waverly with John O'Carroll bottom left and toddler Maureen on right being held by sister Eileen.

While the assembly observed reverent silence, my father would unfurl and raise the Irish tricolor to the accompaniment of a bugler playing "The Last Post".

My mother, who had been decorated by the Irish government for her roles in the 1916 Uprising and the subsequent Black and Tan, and Civil Wars, was given the honor of placing the laurel wreath on the front of the decorated iron gate of the memorial above the bronze shield. As she stepped forward with the wreath, always proudly draped over her left arm was the old grey-green jacket of her Cumann-na-mBan uniform.

For a little girl, the trip and the proceedings to this point were always exciting. But when speeches began and the small Irish group bowed their heads in prayer, it was easy to then become aware of the cold and the length of the ceremony. To calm my fidgeting, I would be passed quietly from one adult to another, "shushed" by comforting voices, with my head patted by weathered hands.

"See the nice, quiet doggie" someone would whisper, pointing discreetly, and indeed, "The Dogs" would always distract me for a while. On either side of the iron gates, mounted on marble pedestals and facing each other, were two graceful bronze Irish wolfhounds.

With each yearly visit I discovered more items of fascination and distraction. On the lovely green and gold mosaic floor of the memorial, I could count the eighteen inlaid shamrocks surrounding a Celtic harp, the national symbol of Ireland, and at the base of the monument, read the words,

Pray for the souls of Michael Dwyer, the Wick-

low Chief, and Mary his wife, whose remains
are interred in this vault.

Sometimes during my father's speech-making, I would slip around to the back of the monument and be absorbed for a long time, tracing with my finger, the hundreds of Celtic-style letters carved into the marble which made up the names of the Irish heroes, many familiar to me.

Though our Easter trips to the Waverly Monument were faithfully observed throughout my childhood, the complement of pilgrims, and the circumstances surrounding the visits, changed. Some of the elderly people who had accompanied us in the earlier years were now dead or unable to make the trip. Furthermore, in Europe, Britain was being threatened with war and Irish Nationalism in Anglo-Australia was not a popular sentiment. Attendance continued to decline. We no longer piled onto the back of Mr. Whelan's truck, but made the long journey by public transportation, first taking the tram into the city, then waiting for the next one to Waverley in the dark and cold at the tram shed at Central Station, all the time carefully protecting the important laurel wreath from the bumps of other early morning passengers, and holding the flag and pole upright, out of harm's way.

Despite my father's zealous determination to maintain the Waverly tradition, there was one bleak year when the assembly only consisted of our immediate family. We could not afford to bring a bugler this time. Instead, as dawn broke, Dad unfurled the flag and cued my sister Cathleen, a gangling eleven year-old. She ascended the sandstone step, raised her violin and bow, and again "The Last Post" was heard at Waverley.

Even though general attendance at the service had wavered at times, the importance of this Irish monument eventually increased over the years, becoming a greater National symbol to more patriots and their descendants.

After my father died, and up to the time of her death in 1988, my mother continued her annual pilgrimage to Waverley, not as she had previously traveled – on the back of the fruit truck and then by public transportation – but now called for in a limousine. Proudly wearing her Irish medals, she would be escorted to Waverly and in the now crowded assembly, given a position of honor.

RUNNING AWAY

As a young girl, I was quite certain that I was misunderstood and unappreciated so I decided to leave home. The trams that passed our house on Darling Street had various destinations posted on the front of the cars, and one of these was the suburb of Leichardt. I knew that Leichardt was a famous explorer who had attempted to cross Australia, suffered extreme hardships and perished in the Outback. He had traveled great distances, so surely this suburb named for him had to be a long way away from my home. I often fantasized about catching the tram there, getting off at the last stop, and living like a gypsy in a cubby house that I would make in the bushes.

I started plotting. Knowing that I would be living in Leichardt until I grew up, I would need a lot of provisions. In our hallway stood an empty old fiber trunk bound in wood and papered in peeling shipping labels. It had originally been sent to us full of clothes, from my Aunt Ellie in London. I dragged it into my room and started filling it. First I packed Topsy, then a towel, some apples, unwrapped Weetbix and all of my clothes. Just for security, I took all of my sisters' clothes too. Loaded as it was, there was no way I could have move it but I didn't think of that.

Neither did I consider the tram schedule or where I would find the money for my fares, but I did put a lot of thought into a suitable farewell note. At the counter in my father's barber shop I took some paper and wrote:

> *Nobody understands me, nobody loves me. I don't want to live here and you won't even notice that I'm gone. You'll be sorry when I'm dead but it will be too late to be nice to me, so good bye!*
>
> *Your loving daughter,*
>
> *Maureen*

Just as I finished writing my father came in and sent me on an errand. I happily did as requested knowing that this would be the last order I would ever have to take, but was gauche enough to leave the incriminating note on the counter in full view.

I innocently returned from the errand to a household that sparked with indignation. It was apparent from the raised, angry voices that greeted me that my father had discovered the note, and my sisters, their barren wardrobe. My epistle was waved in front of my face – "What is all of this nonsense!"

Dodging my father's menacing hand, I fled to the

refuge of my room only to be confronted by two furious sisters. They were harder to dodge.

I had thought all along that my family didn't love and understand me. Now I knew it. I was forced to unpack the trunk and punished for my insulting note. Life was much harder for me than it could have ever been for Ludwig Leichardt.

TOPSY

Topsy was my beloved doll and dear friend. Made of painted plaster, she was black and very pretty, with hair that was molded, limbs that moved, and she wore a blue floral dress. I loved and cared for Topsy. I dressed her, read her stories and tucked her into my bed, but the one maternal gesture I could not make was to bathe her because I had discovered that her paint dissolved in water.

At our school, a raffle was held and my mother bought a ticket. The second and third prizes were a fruit cake made by one of the mothers and a small statue of the Virgin Mary, but the first prize, coveted by all the girls in the school, was a beautiful life-size, celluloid doll. Crowned with a wig of golden curls, with blue eyes and a cupid's bow mouth, she was dressed in a complete set of handmade baby clothing including a crocheted white jacket with lots of ribbons, a bonnet, a silky embroidered dress and dainty booties. She was the most exquisite thing I had ever seen.

The raffle was held and my mother's ticket won the first prize! Mum came to school to collect the doll and, with my sister Pat, I proudly walked home with her, aware of the envious glances of my school mates. At home, Mum sat her prize on the kitchen table admiring it while Pat and I stood by, excited and expectant.

"It's a pretty doll, isn't it?" she said. "A lot of work has gone into making her clothes." She untied its bonnet, "Look at the curls. You'd swear it was human hair, wouldn't you."

My sister and I agreed with her, anxiously waiting for a decision to be made about the doll.

Mother lifted it from the table and said "Maureen, you're the youngest girl so I think you should have this doll."

Pat immediately protested – "That's not fair! She's already got a doll and I haven't."

"No I don't, I don't have a doll" I quickly denied.

"You do so too!"

"I do not!"

The arguing continued "You've got Topsy" Pat insisted.

"No I don't. Topsy died."

My mother, exasperated, halted the bickering, "If this keeps up, neither of you will get the doll. I'll put it away for now and make a decision later."

I had to have that doll and I knew I wouldn't get

her if I still had Topsy. In a frenzy, I rushed to find Topsy and hiding her under my sweater, smuggled her into the laundry room, filled a bucket with water and submerged my helpless doll. As I churned her about, Topsy's paint lifted off, and the plaster from which she was made started to disintegrate in the water, revealing fibrous horse hair underneath. Driven by greed for the blonde temptress, I continued this frantic destruction and then took what was let of mutilated Topsy and wrapped her in newspaper, hiding the sodden corpse at the bottom of the garbage can where it would never be found.

That evening after dinner, my mother called me into her bedroom where she had the new doll propped on a pillow. I listened nervously "Well" she said "I was thinking of giving you this doll. But have you got a doll?"

I glanced at the raffle prize longingly, "No, I don't have a doll."

"But Pat said you did" my mother challenged.

"No, I don't have a doll. I used to but I don't anymore. She's gone."

So I was given the blond beauty. I took her to my room to play, but now she looked different. She wasn't beautiful anymore. She was large and cumbersome and didn't tuck under my arm the way Topsy always did. Her hard china blue eyes looked as malicious as I felt, and guilt overcame me so desperately that I just sat and wept.

I hated her for making me so cruelly betray my loyal friend and I never made her part of my life, but mourned for a very long time the loss of dear Topsy.

BOARDING SCHOOL

I n the girls' adventure stories that I read, the young heroines always went to boarding school. They weren't subjected to the petty disciplines of home life, but were free to lead more exciting lives, hosting secret parties in their dormitory rooms at night, rescuing pet dogs from burning buildings and catching international spies who had taken refuge in the stables on the school grounds. I loved reading about their color- ful experiences as an escape from my own every- day life, shared with irksome brothers and sisters and demanding parents.

When I was troublesome, sometimes my father would threaten me - "Right, you keep this up, just keep it up and I'll send you off to boarding school. Let them take care of you." His warnings bewildered me as I wanted very much to go there anyhow, and so my transgressions were repeated with the hope that he would carry out his threat.

Despite my irritating ways, I wasn't sent to boarding school as punishment, but eventually did go, not because I was naughty or because my parents found the money to send me, but because our house burnt down.

On the occasion of my parents' wedding anniversary, the entire family went to the Hoyts Theater at the top of Darling Street to see a film. It was a very rare occurrence for us to go to the movies *en masse*, but we did that night.

While we sat in the theater watching the film, sirens could be heard outside, and a short time later the manager came in and whispered to my father, who then anxiously told us that we all had to leave the theater. After some muttered words to my mother, he hurried ahead while the rest of us walked down the street bemoaning the fact that we had missed the end of the film.

The complaining was abruptly halted by the shocking sight of fire engines in front of our smoldering house, and firemen in their brass helmets rolling up canvas hoses on the wet pavement. Small groups of neighbors were gathered under the street light and an acrid, smoky smell filled the evening air. We spent that night at a neighbor's house where from the window, we could see our charred home with a fireman on duty pacing outside.

At school the next day, I felt rather important as everyone wanted to know about the fire, and we received lots of attention. I liked this. But after school, when the nuns told me that with my sisters, I would have to spend the night at the convent, the pleasure I took in my celebrity status paled with the sobering reality of the situation.

That evening, we sat in the kitchen of the convent, where the cook gave us cups of tea and a plate of leftover soggy tomato sandwiches. Our refusal to eat them elicited a familiar threat - "If you won't eat them now, you can have them for breakfast." We sat there uneasily until bedtime when a nun escorted us down to a sparsely furnished basement room where the three of us were put into one bed.

In this eerie place, with the inevitable crucifix on the wall above our heads, we cuddled together under the covers cautiously whispering to each other in the dark. Shuffling footsteps crescendoed on the marble steps outside and four nuns entered the room, each holding a candle. We had always heard that nuns shaved their heads, and now before us stood a terrifying quartet of wimpleless nuns, their short hair standing up in spikes and the candlelight illuminating their ghostly faces. They walked around our bed mumbling prayers, and the soporific sounds of their swishing black robes with the clink of rosary beads, made me clench my eyes shut and promise our Heavenly Father that I would be a good girl forever and ever.

The next day we didn't go to school, but waited at the convent where our mother visited us, bringing some clothes donated by neighbors. She explained that while the house was being repaired, we would have to go away to boarding school.

A parish car arrived and took my sisters and

me on a long journey to Narellan, a small country town which had, situated on its rural outskirts, a Catholic girls boarding school and orphanage. It was one of the few times we had ridden in an automobile, and it was the first time I had ever been to the country. I was awed by the isolating quiet of the surroundings and crisp sharpness of the air. We drove in through the open iron gates, the gravel of the wide path crunching under the automobile tires, to a large, modern two-story building of red brick where we were greeted and ushered into the office by two nuns.

Following enrollment procedures, I was led away from my sisters and taken to a dormitory in a separate building which housed other younger girls. Two older prefects showed me my cot and warned me to avoid the partitioned area where a monitoring nun slept at night. That evening, after bedtime prayers, the girl in the neighboring cot whispered "You know where the toilets are, don't you?" and continued "don't try and go there during the night because snakes live in them, and if you go to the loo at night, they'll bite you on the bum."

I didn't usually get up at night to go to the toilet, but now I lay in bed terrified of having to go, and the fear of a snake rearing its head and biting me on the bum was more than I could handle. At some stage during the night, I wet the bed.

The custom at Narellan was for punishments

118

to be dealt out before breakfast, when the entire school was assembled in the dining room. While we sat at our benches waiting to eat, the list of offenders was read out. I was marched up to the rostrum where a nun wielding a cane bellowed out my name and crime – "Maureen O'Carroll wet the bed." I was caned on the spot. I had never been caned before and was demeaned and embarrassed.

My mortification didn't end there. Each young child had a monitor, an older girl who was responsible for her. So when a child committed a "crime", her monitor was also caned. This pecking order resulted in the inevitable. After breakfast, my furious monitor cornered me, meting out her own slaps. The vicious cycle continued – of avoiding the snakes, being caned, having the monitor caned, and then copping a cuffing from her.

My experience at boarding school so far was nothing like what I had read about in my adventure stories and I was lonely and miserable. Furthermore, I was hungry. The meals were spartan and the country air had sharpened my appetite. The best food was at recess, when one of the nuns brought to our play yard a basket full of coarse slabs of white bread, spread thickly with golden syrup. But our three unappetizing meals, eaten in the dining hall, included such offerings as lumpy gruel, overcooked vegetables and meat, tasteless stewed fruit and burnt custard. Always accompanying these meals was a mug of watery milk which was from the convent dairy, but before it could nourish us, all traces of cream had been removed by the nuns to make butter.

Smarter girls supplemented their diet with illicit raids on the nearby fields of vegetables and watermelons. I was proud and excited to be included once in such a group, who after climbing over a fence, broke open watermelons and scooped the delicious pink pulp out with their hands.

Corn also grew nearby, and we were sometimes permitted to pluck an ear and scrape off the kernels. Most of us had managed to acquire a tobacco tin and we would light a small fire in a field, and putting a few kernels in them, we would place our precious tins in the embers. This was my introduction to popcorn and one of my happy memories of boarding school. The magic of the few kernels popping and then the excitement of eating them by the open fire gave me great pleasure.

Less pleasurable was the morning bathing ritual. The school had a collection of woolen neck-to-knee swimming costumes that looked as though they had been donated by a bathing society from the Twenties. Each girl was issued one as part of her uniform along with a school dress, a play dress and a good dress used for Sunday Mass and parents' visits. Before breakfast, in the frosty early morning, we had to jog in our ill-fitting swimsuits to the Nepean River and jump up and down in the cold water. Our escort was a nun bundled up in layers of her warm habit who supervised our ablutions until she was sure we were all completely soaked and thoroughly miserable. Wet and shivering, we ran even faster back to school.

Rarely did I see my sisters during my stay at Narellan, but Cathleen, having arranged the Mendelssohn Spring Song for violin, cello and piano, cleverly organized for us to have periodic rehearsals. The nuns were thrilled to have a trio to perform for the all-important visit of the Archbishop, and we in turn were happy to escape some of the daily misery of boarding school.

Our parents visited on alternate Sundays with a treat for each of us, a bag of boiled sweets. Every time, I planned that my bag would last for the entire week, but invariably, larger, shrewder girls surrounded me as soon as my parents had left. "Oh, what do you have there? You're going to share with us, aren't you?" Nothing inspires generosity more than a gang of threatening-looking girls. Their companionship however, only lasted until the last lick of the lollies.

I spent three months at Narellan and most of the time I was bitterly homesick. Segregated as we were, I missed the comfort and company of my older sisters. I missed too, my annoying brothers, and I missed all the other people I had wanted to get away from all my life.

Finally though, the exciting day arrived when my parents came to take us home to our newly-renovated house. The fire had not burnt our brick terrace to the ground, but had only gutted the inside, and oddly enough, it had been rebuilt and even painted in exactly the same fashion as it was before. Nothing had changed – the rooms were as tiny, the staircase had the same creaks, and the color scheme too was unchanged, only the paint was fresher.

Now I cherished being home in familiar surroundings with all the reassurances of routine family life. My brothers arrived back from their boarding school and a new kind of bond developed between all of us where in for a long time afterwards, we took pleasure in comparing notes on our respective boarding school experiences.

PURCELL SWEETS

S aturday mornings were always spent at the Conservatorium of Music. I had my cello lesson with Mr. Bell, followed by a half hour music theory class. When I was eight, I was accepted into the elementary orchestra, a string group of beginning players conducted by William Krasnik, a very fine musician and a gentle, patient teacher.

I enjoyed his orchestra but was never particularly aware of the compositions we were playing. It's only when one is more sophisticated that the composer's name is recognized rather than just the notes.

One Saturday morning at the end of our rehearsal, Mr. Krasnik said "You have all played wonderfully today. I'm proud of the work you're doing. In fact, you are playing so well that next week I'm going to bring you some Purcell Suites."

He was of course referring to the composer, Henry Purcell.

However, I was more familiar with the billboards that advertised Pascall Sweets. I didn't know what a suite of music was. A sweet to me was a lolly. I had had Pascall Sweets a few times and absolutely loved them. They were like a Viensese Bon Bon – hard on the outside with a fruity, chewy center. Comparatively expensive, one of them cost the same amount as six or seven humbugs, so they were a very special treat.

I was excited all week with the prospect of my good work being rewarded with Pascall Sweets! The next Saturday at orchestra, I was in my seat early, with my bow rosined, my cello tuned, and I was going to play as well as possible.

The orchestra rehearsal always lasted for one hour. Mr. Krasnik distributed the music and proceeded to conduct. I followed the notes, reading the music as carefully as I could but the hour seemed to be interminable. When will he give us the Pascall sweets he promised! Finally, Mr. Krasnik stopped conducting and tapped the music stand with his baton – "Well girls and boys, that was very good reading. Now practice your music during the week and I will see you next Saturday. Thank you."

I couldn't contain myself any longer. I had tried so hard and I hadn't gotten my Pascall sweets. Loud sobs burst from me with a stream of tears. As the bewildered conductor turned to me, I cried "Mr. Krasnik, you are a mean, mean man!" and ran out of the hall.

The poor man never found out the source of my

grief and the great pity was that I stopped liking him, and in fact, mistrusted him. I couldn't forgive him for not bringing me the promised Pascall sweets, but when, years later in another orchestra, as a more sophisticated cellist, I read the title and composer of a work we were playing – "Suite, by Henry Purcell" – I was saddened to realize how youth and ignorance had separated me from a fine and caring mentor.

MY LIFE AS A PRINCESS

Once upon a time I was a princess. My brothers and sisters had contracted diphtheria and were ensconced in the isolation hospital, and I had my parents all to myself. With great ease, I assumed the role of an only child.

It was a dramatic day when my father lined us up in the backyard and in the bright sunlight, using the handle of a spoon as a tongue depressor, critically examined our throats. Dad methodically wiped the spoon with an alcohol swab as he went from child to child. He suspected diphtheria, a dangerous but reasonably common illness before the days of vaccination, as some of the children were ill and feverish. Our local physician, Doctor Cable, was sent for and confirming my father's suspicion, ordered an ambulance.

Observed by curious neighbors, we all piled into the box-shaped white vehicle marked with a red cross. I didn't have a sore throat and felt fine, so unlike my ailing brothers and sisters who appeared to be suffering the journey, I peered out the back window and found the long bumpy ride very exciting as we drove to Prince Henry Hospital at La Perouse. This was the isolation hospital located on a bleak, windswept point of Botany Bay where hapless convicts had first landed and where now, infected patients were quarantined.

We were taken into the stark, disinfectant-reeking emergency room where white-coated doctors examined us and swabbed our throats. I had enjoyed the ride and the attention thus far, but took no pleasure in being forced to gag on a cotton covered stick. Despite my father's entreaties to "sit still and be a good girl" my sense of self-protection guaranteed that the doctors and nurses would pay for this indignity with scratches. To their relief, I was the only child without diphtheria and after the others were wheeled away to the isolation ward, I took my father's hand and triumphantly accompanied him out of Prince Henry Hospital.

On the long tram ride home, Dad explained to me about the severity of the illness that had stricken my siblings and soberly informed me that the doctors expected them to be in the hospital for a long time. I shared his concern, but as an eight year-old, had a different point of view. Sitting alone with my father, it occurred to me that I was even now, as a result of diphtheria and the fate of my own good health, beginning to fulfill the fantasy that I had so often indulged in – that of being an Only Child.

I was not disappointed in my promotion to this

new role, and the freedom, appreciation and indulgences that came with it. For the first time in my life, I not only had my parents to myself, but also the undivided attention of my adult sister and brother, Eileen and Emmett, who were staying with us at the time. I was allowed to join in the conversation at the dinner table. I was offered second helpings and given treats like cake and lollies. My hair was curled and be-ribboned. I had the soapy bathtub all to myself, and could wear my sisters' clothes without having to ask their permission. It is possible that besides worrying about their sick children, my parents were concerned that I would be bereft and lonely without my brothers and sisters, so indulged me in this manner.

My father treated me to a midday dinner at the Hyde Park Hotel. Attired in Cathleen's best dress, I sat at a table which was covered with a starched white linen table cloth, a puzzling array of shiny silverware and more sparkling glasses than we had in our whole cupboard at home! An attentive waiter wearing a cropped jacket with a linen napkin draped over his arm, brought me a glass of raspberry soda, and after the traditional baked dinner, offered for dessert, steaming plum pudding with custard – a delicacy that was usually only served at home at Christmas time. And once, Eileen took me to the movie theatre where we sat in the stalls, saw *Gulliver's Travels*, and bought a paper cup full of Peters Ice Cream at intermission. Afterwards, we had afternoon tea at Cahill's coffee shop. I just relished my life.

At night when I said my prayers, I always suggested to God that it would be a good idea if He took all of my sick brothers and sisters to Heaven to live with Him, so that they wouldn't need to come home, and I could remain an only child forever.

Even on the occasion when I accompanied my parents to the hospital at La Perouse, I had an experience that could not have occurred had all of my brothers and sisters been with me.

Children were not allowed to visit the hospital so while my parents were there, I was free to wander around the open, sandy scrubland that fronted the ocean at Botany Bay. At that time, the only Aborigines visible near Sydney were at La Perouse where they carved and sold boomerangs and demonstrated their skill in throwing them. This day I was gazing covetously at the displays of boomerangs and trinkets when the old Aboriginal vendor offered in his broken English to teach me how to throw one of his boomerangs. On that windswept, sandy knoll, with his blue-black hand steadying my child's wrist, he guided my arm until it had gained enough momentum to release the boomerang. With a singing sound, it sailed through the clear air, it's spinning v-shape silhouetted against the brilliant blue sky, and as I gasped at the wonder of it all, it gave a final hiss and landed on the ground near me. The chuckle of the lean and grizzled Aborigine, his tight grin displaying absent front teeth, and my own victorious sensation as I looked down at the boomerang spent from flight, has remained with me as part of my own Dreamtime.

When my parents emerged from the hospital after their visit, I made the obligatory inquiry, "How are they?"

Then anticipating their reply "I'm terribly sorry to have to tell you, but they have left us and gone to Heaven. So now Maureen, you are the only child left in the family."

This was not the reply. They didn't go to heaven. They came home and they ruined my charmed life.

That awful day, when my brothers and sisters returned, brought an abrupt end to my reign as the Only Child.

I was kept busy helping my mother with preparations for the invalids, "Here, run downstairs and get a blanket, run upstairs and get a pillow. Stop dawdling, I need your help right now!"

I made a meteoric descent from princess to servant and was sent running back and forth with their meals, flasks of water, comic books and dirty dishes. I even had to empty their chamber pot! I resented them terribly.

I still prayed every night that they would leave us and go to heaven. But they didn't. They recovered – and I became an agnostic.

WORLD WAR TWO

I t was my seventh birthday on September 3, 1939 when Great Britain and France declared war on Germany after its invasion of Poland two days earlier.

The start of another war was cause for grave concern as the terrible sacrifices that had been made in World War I by young Australian men, in the name of the British Empire, were well remembered. However, when World War II first broke out, Australia was far from the European conflict, and the distance and isolation of the continent, for the most part, initially insulated her people from first-hand awareness and suffering. In our own family, we were fortunate not to ever experience any wartime losses, and for a young child, the changes brought about by the War only made life more interesting and exciting.

As children, we were given a special sense of importance by participating in "Austerity Programs" which encouraged recycling of all sorts of material for the war effort. The inclination for children to collect odds and ends became more than a casual occupation when the pursuit was not only actively encouraged by adults, but our contributions were going to win the war! Games were replaced with scavenger hunts for materials such as tin foil and even the smallest amounts were treasured. The shiny tops of milk bottles were prized as were chocolate wrappers and cigarette packaging and family cupboards were quickly stripped of their stored tinsel Christmas ornaments. The previously ignored garbage cans as well as street gutters became treasure troves for dedicated young scavengers and as we deposited our collective finds in bins at the front of the classrooms, our reward was the words of praise from school teachers and the childlike assumption that all Allied bullets and tanks were made from our chocolate wrappers and milk bottle tops.

Scraps of wool and bits of fluff were also gathered for recycling, to be turned into felt, and old woolen items were unraveled to knit warm socks and mittens for soldiers and European refugees. Occasionally our zealousness was met with anger and frustration by Mum as she would discover buttons, "collected for the war effort", missing from garments and even once, a necessary school sweater, reduced to a ball of yarn.

The possibility of war reaching our shores first became apparent to us when the Balmain Town Hall clock, a visible target for potential bombers, was dismantled "for the duration".

Prior to the War an airplane rarely appeared in the skies, but now the sight and sound of them became more common. Daily, we heard on the radio frightening stories of "Hitler bombing London", and so when I heard a plane overhead at night, I envisioned that there was a little man with a finger moustache and dark hair slanted across his forehead, sitting in the cockpit. Terrified, I would hide under the blankets pleading – "Please Mr. Hitler, don't drop a bomb on us." Mr. Hitler's bombs offered no immediate danger to a little girl hiding under the covers in Balmain, but as the war continued and Australia was under serious threat of invasion, not by the Germans, but by the Japanese, my pleading at night was transferred to another villain – "Please Mr. Tojo, don't drop a bomb on us."

With the increasing threat of Japanese invasion, the government decided that public air raid shelters and trenches should be dug, and wherever possible families should also build their own. Our air raid shelter was constructed in the back yard utilizing the existing sandstone wall, and with my father acting as overseer, we industriously filled burlap bags with sand to pile up on the tin roof. The shelter was then stocked with emergency provisions – candles, some stone jugs of water and a large sealed tin of Arnott's Arrowroot Biscuits which we all eyed gluttonously.

The challenge of building an air raid shelter was gloriously met by our neighbor, Mary MacQuaid, a 90 year-old Irish lady who dug and constructed entirely by herself, a covered trench in her back-yard. She laid little steps down to this shelter and used sheets of corrugated tin to line the walls and make the roof, over which she hauled sandbags. My father, extremely impressed by this remarkable feat, took us all to Mary MacQuaid's yard to show us this shelter and to point out that if a 90 year-old lady could accomplish this single-handedly, what marvelous things we could achieve if we were "less slothful" and applied ourselves to a task the way Mary MacQuaid had. We patiently suffered his lecturing as we too were very impressed by this shelter, and decided that if we were more sociable to our neighbor, she would probably let us play in her wonderful new cubby house, especially as we weren't allowed to play in our own shelter.

When we eventually did have an air raid drill, it was at night, and we were hurried from our beds to the shelter where, wrapped in blankets, we sat silently in candle light, excited but also a little cold and scared. After a while, the whine of the "all clear" siren sounded and my parents reassured us that everything was all right and we could now go back to bed. But my brother, Sean, who was very little, started to sob uncontrollably, crying "It's not fair. It wasn't a real air raid because we didn't eat the Arnott's Biscuits."

The war effort had also provided us with a new and exciting playground when an elaborate warren of open air raid trenches was dug in Gladstone Park. They were wide enough to offer quite a challenge when, after a running start, we leapt over them, and deep enough to hurt shins and feet when our jumping skills failed us. During heavy rains, the trenches quickly filled with water which turned a thick muddy yellow from the dense, clay soil and the edges of the trenches became dangerously slippery, making our leaping games all the more daring.

On one occasion, every youngster in Balmain had a special wartime memento. A number of wooden crates packed with gas masks had washed up and broke open on the rocky waterfront near the Balmain Baths. Dozens and dozens of gas masks had floated loose from the splintered crates and now littered the shore. They were discovered by some boys and the story of this momentous find quickly spread like a bushfire, and every child who was ambulatory high-tailed it to the park edge before the next tide came in, to claim as their own, one of these incredible souvenirs. No pirate captain had ever discovered such a beach full of treasures! Each mask had a canvas hood, bug-like eye goggles and an accordion rubber hose to cover the mouth and nose. They were stained with globs of oil from the polluted water and stank with a musty smell that spoke of old rubber and long storage, but they were an exciting, sophisticated find.

With our usual display of good sense, we each pulled a mask on over our head and face and after spending some play time trying to scare each other with muffled yells from behind this strange visage, we walked home, pleased with the startled looks of passersby and confident that our parents would be amused to see us so uniquely garbed. 'Twas not so. They were only humorless and carried on about silly children who didn't have the sense not to pick up on beaches filthy things that had been "who knows where", and put them on their faces, "making a holy show of themselves all over the neighborhood."

The gas masks were confiscated and our faces and heads, roughly scrubbed. To make matters worse, some of the wiser beachcombers, who had less faith than we did in their parents' ability to recognize a true treasure, continued to parade and play with their gas masks in front of us making our loss all the more galling.

RATIONING

F ood rationing was introduced during the War and for many families this presented a hardship. There was a strict limit on the amount of butter that could be purchased in any one week. Sugar was rationed so the housewife who made her own jams and baked cakes was constrained, and more luxurious meats like steak and lamb chops were also restricted. Ration coupon books for these various foods were distributed but because of the nature of our diet, these restrictions were of little consequence to our family.

The rationing of butter didn't affect us because it rarely graced the bread in our household but instead, we always had in the kitchen, a large roasting pan full of beef dripping. Accumulated from baking meats, it served as a shortening in scones and dumplings, was used and reused to fry eggs, liver and onions, bake roasts and vegetables, and finally, when it had absorbed the flavors of all these foods, it became the spread for our daily bread. The firm surface was a deep chestnut color, sometimes studded with bits of meat and onions, and when its crust was broken, ruby rich shiny jelly could be scooped from underneath the dripping, and both, thickly spread on a piece of bread with a liberal sprinkling of salt, provided a complete and most delicious meal.

We also had sugar coupons frequently left over to trade with neighbors or use as gifts. Tea drinking was introduced at a very young age in our house and sugar was primarily used to sweeten the endless cups that we drank. (When a child was old enough to be weaned, his liquid supplement became weak tea, and was then neutralized with an inch or so of milk.) As my mother didn't bake, and the jam in our house came from "Old Judge" tins, there was still plenty of rationed sugar left for the morning bowl of porridge.

Meat was rationed on a point system. The most popular and expensive meats – roasts, steaks, and lamb chops – used up coupons very quickly, but organ meats such as liver, kidneys, brains and tripe, were very inexpensive and required few coupons. A typical dinner for us was a practical one-pot meal such as tripe and onions served over boiled potatoes with white sauce, brains simmered in milk and served on toast (with a portion set aside to be mashed up for the baby), fried liver or kidneys, or a great pot of thick stew using a variety of vegetables and ox tails or marrow bones or a meat combination bought by the pound, poetically called "Butcher's Special". This was not "wartime" food for us but our regular fare, and represented the limited cooking skills, economizing ways and preferred tastes that my parents had brought with them from Ireland.

They also brought form Ireland - probably as a result of childhood deprivation - a very great respect for the availability of food, and a firm intolerance of any wastage of it. My mother had experienced extreme poverty as a child after her father, while working as a builder, fell from the roof of a Dublin Hospital and was crippled – in an era when compensation and insurance were very rare. She told us of how she and her five siblings would be put to bed for the day and told to lie still so as to conserve their energy, when there was no coal or food in the house.

In sunny Australia, we had no concept of how bitterly cold an unheated house must have been in a Dublin winter, and in our sufficiently-fed state, we also had little understanding of why, after rejecting food on our plate, it was set aside and served again at the next mealtime, and we would not be offered any other food until these leftovers were eaten.

From her grandparents, my mother had heard heart-breaking stories of entire families, after being evicted from their simple homes during the Irish Potato Famine, starving to death by the roadside. With us, she commonly used an expression from that time – "You'll follow a crow for that" – when she saw any food wasted. Again, it was hard for us to imagine how anyone could be so hungry that they would chase a crow for the crust of bread it might have in its beak.

While rationing wasn't severe in Australia and people could supplement supplies with bartered ration coupons or goods, there was a strong awareness and concern for the harsh food shortages being experienced by relatives and friends in England and other parts of Europe. My father regularly sent to Aunt Elly and Uncle James in England, tea, sugar, and jam and when available, canned fish. He also sent eggs and had a very clever way of shipping them. After dipping the eggs in water glass, a preservative, he gently pushed each one into the ever-versatile beef dripping that had been scooped into a cake tin. Completely surrounded by the solid fat, the eggs were well cushioned from breakage, and as an extra precaution, my father wrapped and stitched the tin in many layers of burlap. They always arrived unbroken and his sister and brother could enjoy the rarely available eggs and also a necessary fat supplement.

My father's inventiveness with eggs didn't end there. Dad was in his forties when the war broke out and for a while he was in the army, stationed at a base outside of Sydney. He was assigned the duties of breakfast cook. Large quantities of fresh eggs often weren't available for the soldiers, and so powdered eggs were used. It was the custom that before breakfast, one of the men would go by the kitchen to see what sorts of eggs were being cooked and then report back to the others. This information became the deciding factor as to whether or not they ate the cooked eggs. Realizing the importance of fresh eggs to the soldiers, Dad collected and saved a large box of broken eggshells. He would bring them into the kitchen in the morning and scatter them about in a casual fashion on the countertop. A head would peek around the corner, then disappear and Dad would hear down the hallway – "Hey, we get fresh eggs today!" The men would then all turn up for a breakfast of scrambled eggs, voicing none of the usual complaints about the powdery consistency. Dad toted the box of eggshells around for the duration of the War and took great pleasure in telling the story of the soldiers and the eggs.

ANCHOR TO SHIP

In August of 1941, a dastardly deed was committed on Darling Street in Balmain. The resident hawker of the Anchor Hairdressing Salon was abducted – our parrot had been pinched! My parents, who had always denied that they were superstitious, nevertheless regarded this incident as a sign of impending change. As it was, many changes had already occurred. With my father and Uncle John away in the Army, Mother not only took care of all of us, but also assumed the responsibilities of the Anchor Hairdressing Salon. However, with both men absent and many customers now receiving army haircuts, no barbering was done and our income from the business was considerably reduced, although my mother did manage to maintain the tobacco concession as well as the gift counter – and also the lending library.

Following the parrot's disappearance – as fate would have it – the terrace house and business next door at 218 Darling Street were offered for sale. My parents purchased them. The house was the same size and configuration as the one we lived in at 220, and the shop, which had previously sold fruit, also occupied as much floor space as The Anchor did. They opened a "mixed business" at 218 selling milk, confectionery, canned goods and other convenience groceries, and christened it "The Ship".

Although 218 was the same size as 220, as it was during Wartime, this type of business was more practical than the Anchor because it wasn't reliant on men's hairdressing for income. It was also one that, if necessary, my mother could operate by herself. The residence at 220 was rented out, The Anchor was closed down, and the novels of Disraeli and Lytton donated to the public library.

Our possessions were then moved next door without any drama, except for the large upright piano which would not fit through any of the doorways. Applying the collective wisdom of the gathering crowd of observers on the footpath, the moving men eventually buckled the piano into large straps, and supported on the backs of two of them, it was hoisted up and through one of the upstairs front windows. Then after failed attempts to maneuver it down the narrow staircase, a decision was finally made that the front bedroom would become the music room and my parents would convert the living room downstairs into their bedroom.

This move from The Anchor to The Ship, although only from one doorway to the next, introduced many changes in our lives, our mother's life, and in her relationship to us. With my father absent, a shift occurred in all of our roles, most notably our mother's and a new balance was established in the family wherein we had the opportunity to get to know her better.

For extended periods during the War, Mum single-handedly ran The Ship. Being a very social person with a good business sense, she enjoyed the interaction with customers and having the freedom to take charge of the shop, and indeed the household, without the interference of a dominating man. With her children now older, she could better utilize their help, and she made the tasks attractive enough so that we enjoyed weighing out pound bags of sugar, slicing cheese, stocking shelves and making milkshakes and ice cream sundaes. The mathematics learned at school now became rewarding with practical application in the shop when tallying up costs, weighing out bulk groceries and stocktaking. I took particular pride in accurately adding up the long columns of bookkeeping each night with ever-increasing speed.

The change in business in fact made many aspects of life easier for Mother. For the first time, she had access to refrigeration. Previously, we had to purchase daily our supply of fresh food, but now had the convenience of being able to keep provisions in the large commercial refrigerator in the shop which also gave us ready access to milk, cheese and other chilled items, and storage for leftovers. While my parents had always managed to keep some canned goods on hand, the cost and the physical limitations of carrying them home with other groceries kept the supply small. But now we displayed on the shelves of our shop, many dozens of cans of various foods – soups, meats, baked beans and stewed fruit, all purchased wholesale and conveniently delivered to the door in a large van.

Mother never took for granted, but expressed pleasure in, the ease with which she could prepare a quick meal for us with a can of tomato soup diluted with milk and served with slices of toast, or the simplicity of using toast again as a base for baked beans, rationed fish or bully beef, all quickly available with the twist of a can opener.

Sometimes on washing day, which was now changed from the traditional Monday to Sunday because of the hours of The Ship, Mum acquiesced to our pleas and took from the top shelf in our shop, one of the cans of sweetened condensed milk. With feigned ignorance, she always insisted, "Why would you want to put this perfectly good tin of condensed milk in the bottom of the copper, to boil away with the sheets and towels?"

"Just wait, Mum. Let us show you" we would plead. "You'll see what happens to it!"

At the end of the long washing day – unable to disguise our presumption that unlike us, our mother had never done anything adventurous –

146

we triumphantly retrieved and then opened the long-stewed tin of sweetened milk which by now had turned into a solid brown cylinder of delicious caramel. While Mum generously expressed surprise and wonder at our culinary talents, we took turns levering out shiny spoonfuls of the tanned confection, discarding the pristine tin only when the strongest of index fingers could no longer encourage any trace of caramel taste from its interior.

Mother learned more than the art of caramel-making from her Sunday washing days. The open criticism of neighbors and a visit from the priest, impressed upon her the impropriety of toiling in this obvious manner on the Lord's Day. After initial defiance and insistence on her own use of her time, she finally yielded to social dictates and so had to toil even harder on her one day away from the business, by first stacking all the freshly-washed laundry and then waiting until early Monday morning to peg it out on the clothesline.

Dad's absence also meant that Mother had more opportunity to be solely alone with us in the evenings which often led to impromptu story-telling, and on these occasions she frequently harkened back to her days as a teenage girl in Ireland. She would tell us of how – when acting as a Citizen Army messenger with important documents concealed in the tire of her bicycle – she once had been in an accident. A kind British officer put her bike on the back of his truck and drove the upset young girl and her damaged bicycle – complete with secret documents – to her requested destination.

Mum spoke of other adventures with humor too. During the Irish Civil War, she was ordered to smuggle a Gladstone bag full of small munitions via train from Dublin to an outlying town. On arrival, she was horrified to see at the station, a blockade of soldiers searching everybody's luggage. Nervously walking along the platform, she had the good fortune to recognize one of the Irish officers and so made a great fuss of him, expressing pleasure at again seeing an old friend. Flattered, he gallantly offered to carry her bag, "Heavens May!" he exclaimed "What have you got in this bag to make it so heavy?"

"Oh sure" she explained "It's jars of jam my Mam is having me bring to my Grandmother, and you're right, they're very heavy, aren't they."

Her escort graciously gave Mother his arm and carried the bag, unexamined, through the barrier.

So it was during the War that we had this special time with Mother when we got to learn more about her past, her courage and her adventures. We also became aware of a creative side to Mum that she didn't often have a chance to express, though there were times when we didn't appreciate it.

Traditionally on Christmas day, while our parents cooked at the hot stove despite the searing summer temperatures, we went swimming at the Balmain Baths all morning and in the afternoon, would come home tired, sun burnt and hungry to feast on our Christmas dinner which at that time, was virtually the same fare in all households – a roast of meat with baked vegetables and gravy, a dessert of steamed plum pudding with a hot custard sauce and often, dried fruits, nuts and fruitcake to follow. But our innovative Mother, this one wartime Christmas, sent us swimming and when we returned for our traditional baked dinner, we were appalled to see the table set with plates of chilled sliced leg ham, assorted pickles, stuffed eggs, cold potatoes spiced with raw onion, and beetroot which had been simmered in sweetened vinegar, chilled, and then cradled in leaves of crisp lettuce. An unappreciative wail went up "This isn't our Christmas dinner!" My hot, tired and crestfallen mother swore that she would never again attempt to do anything thoughtful for such a bunch of selfish, ungrateful heathens.

But of course, she did. Likewise, she was thoughtful and compassionate towards many of the young women in the area. Most local men were now in the Armed Forces and away the majority of the time, only home for quick leaves – and for some, quick romances. An exuberant young woman would sometimes then visit our shop and share with Mother, joy over her new-found love. When this happened, we were quickly sent into the house as the topic of romance was considered unsuitable for our ears. And we were just as swiftly dismissed when the same woman, a couple of months later, perhaps returned weeping, to quietly confide in my sympathetic mother.

On more than one occasion, Mum was known to have a long sobering talk to a young serviceman and if events worked out as she was determined, we were then sent on short notice to one of the local churches to play "The Bridal March" and "Ave Maria" for a quiet, hastily arranged wedding.

THE YANKEES ARE COMING

Prior to the War, we didn't know any Americans, and our only impression of them came from glamorous Hollywood movies where they were always smartly dressed, went to nightclubs, had lots of money, shiny white teeth, amusing accents and referred to everything as "swell". And we were not disappointed in our perception of them when, after the United States entered the war, their servicemen were stationed in Australia and we finally got to meet some of them. A shipload of American soldiers was anchored at a wharf near us in Balmain, and as these men strolled up Darling Street in their crisp, well-tailored beige uniforms, we noticed their confident style and observed them with a sense of curiosity. They were very tall and tanned, often chewing gum, and spoke loudly, but politely. I'd never before heard women addressed as "Ma'am" and men so frequently called "Sir".

In a very short time, our shop became a congregating area for many of these servicemen, not only because we were conveniently located to the wharf, selling food and snacks, but also my father, who was home at the time, had approached the first Americans he saw, asking them what was typical American food. By the time the first group of soldiers passed our shop, there was already a blackboard outside with the chalked message – "We Sell Hot Dogs". While the hot dogs we offered probably didn't match the style and taste of true American ones, the servicemen continued to frequent "The Ship" and many of them – some very young and undoubtedly homesick – enjoyed chats with Mum and her maternal concern for them, sharing their letters from home, and showing her photos of their faraway families and girlfriends.

As their social life developed and an evening in the city or Kings Cross was planned, they often entrusted their wallets to Mother when she expressed apprehension about "flashing a lot of money around", returning the next day to collect them, and we grew used to seeing the drawer under the cash register filled with American wallets every Saturday evening. As my mother got to know these young men better, she was saddened and concerned when they told her that they were to leave Sydney and be shipped out to the war zones in the Pacific.

These likeable American men, so handsome and outgoing, piqued our schoolgirl curiosity, not only because of their accents and mannerisms, but for other reasons too.

At our house, sloping down from the second story into the back yard was a narrow access ramp which had a solid wooden hand railing on either side of it. My sister Pat and I claimed these railings as our own, and tying a short rope at the end of each one to serve as a bridle, we used to sit on them, pretending that they were our "horses". When we had the opportunity to be alone together, we would say "Let's go sit on the horses". Each straddling one of these railings holding our makeshift reins, we would play games and talk together, all the while, from this elevated position, casually observing the activities in the other yards and street below us.

One day, Pat suggested we sit on our horses, adding excitedly "I want to show you something that Americans do."

We mounted our steeds and my sister pointed to a house on the corner and with a sly smile said "Wait till you see what's going on in that window!"

I looked across and we could clearly see the young blonded woman who lived there embracing an American soldier! This was just like the movies. But after a while, unlike anything we had even seen in the movies, the affectionate couple started to take off each other's clothes. Because of the height of their window sill, they were only visible to these two goggle-eyed schoolgirls from the waist up, but even this limited view of the bare-chested lovers was more than we had ever hoped to see. We had once asked our mother about sex and her terse answer was "the less you know about all that, the better off you'll be in the long run."

Now we had a perfect opportunity to find out about "all that", and were speechless and afraid to blink in case we missed even a second of these grown-up gyrations. Alas, the couple suddenly seemed to sink and disappear below the level of the censoring window sill.

We waited impatiently for a long time but they didn't appear again and with disappointment, we finally abandoned our vigil.

Later in the day, when I was sent down the street on an errand, I saw our blonde neighbor at her door, and the American soldier, now fully clothed, leaving her house with a very circumspect farewell. But I knew better, and with an air of superiority, took pleasure in being the center of attention on the playground the following week as I related the story of my voyeurism, and my newfound knowledge about the special activities of American men.

MARGARET MORNINGTON

Although the two Balmain houses where we lived during my childhood were small for the number of people they accommodated, we still, most of the time, had another person living under our roof. Often a young woman from the country shared the girls' bedroom and worked as a mother's helper. During the Depression, young women wanting to move to the city were willing to work very hard just for a bed, simple meals, and a roof over their head. Not only did they have to cope with their share of household tasks and the constant demands of children, but they were also subjected to the strict rules of conduct insisted upon by my parents.

One of these mother's helpers often took me to Birchgrove Park, walking this long distance through the back streets full of tiny workers' cottages, and pushing the sturdy pram which held my two baby brothers. She used to meet a young man there and they would sit together on the bench, holding hands and chatting, all the while keeping an eye on her charges. Dressed in worker's clothes and wearing a cap, he was probably on his lunch break, and always gave me a small, white paper bag twisted closed at the top. When I opened it, I would find inside a few licorice allsorts which kept me happily occupied while I sat on the swing and separated the layers of licorice and sweet coloured fillings, slowly eating them. I was shrewd enough never to mention this little bribe when I arrived home.

As there were parks much closer to our house, the frequency of these journeys must have aroused my father's suspicion, and one day he unexpectedly appeared at Birchgrove Park and confronted the young couple. In a thunderous voice, he ordered the protesting man to leave, and implying sinful neglect, dismissed the nursemaid, ignoring her desperate promises that it would never happen again.

My righteous father stood by his resolution, and hard as the work was, and as strict as the rules were, she was quickly replaced by another young woman equally anxious to escape the harsh country life to live in the city.

Domineering as he was, my father met his match only once. It was a time when we were very young and my mother was quite ill and hospitalized, so instead of employing a mother's helper, Dad hired an older woman to work as a live-in housekeeper. Her name was Mrs. Betts. She too was from the country, and was as tough as the conditions that she had undoubtedly left. Always dressed in a shapeless floral cotton frock protected by an apron, her frizzed grey hair restrained by a net, and wearing on her bare feet, worn down shoes, she ran the home in a very strict manner, making no concession to my father's usual role as head of the household. In fact, this woman appeared to so sufficiently intimidate him that he left her completely in charge and stayed well clear of her path.

She kept the house agonizingly spotless, attacking every previously undisturbed dusty corner, pouncing on every spot of grease and assaulting every available surface with pungent disinfectant. Large, hearty meals were prepared by Mrs. Betts and she insisted that they be eaten in complete silence, which was quite tolerable as we didn't normally chatter much at the table anyhow, and the food was a marked improvement on my father's cooking. But we were made miserable by her bedtime routine. She would fill the large, concrete laundry sink with soapy water and quickly dunk each of us in, one at a time, roughly scrubbing us with her weathered hands, and as she pulled a reddened child out, she would plunge another one into the graying water. Quickly dressed, we were then put to bed and standing over us, spittle shooting from her dentures, she would snarl, "Go to sleep now. I don't want any nonsense from youse kids!" and clomp down the stairs.

But we knew from experience that she was capable of then creeping noiselessly back up the staircase. At that time, I shared a bed with my two sisters and the three of us would lie there breathlessly, wondering if the dragon was hovering outside the door. After a long wait, one of us would whisper "Do you think she's there?"

In a flash, a thin wooden plank wielded by Mrs. Betts would descend on the covers, "I told youse kids to go to sleep!"

Fortunately, we were blessed with a healthy sense of suspicion and good reflexes, so as the board swished towards us, three sets of arms and legs would instantly push the cover up and away from the bodies, and the plank would land harmlessly on the taut blanket.

Eventually my mother returned from the hospital and was pleasantly surprised to see her house so clean and organized, and find her children so quiet and well-behaved. Mrs. Betts flurried around, attending to last minute details, but then suddenly reached out and gave each of us an unexpected hug. She tempered this show of affection with another one of her choice remarks "Youse kids better be good for your mum or I'll come back and thrash you!"

We soberly watched Mrs. Betts pack her cardboard suitcase and put on her cloth hat and coat for the last time in our house. She took the short walk to the tram stop and moments later, when we looked out the window, the waiting bench was already vacant.

✳ ✳ ✳

One afternoon in my early teen years, my mother and I were weighing out pound bags of dates in our shop when a woman came in hauling a large suitcase with both hands. She put the heavy case down and smiled hopefully at my mother, asking "Do you remember me, May?"

Mum was taken aback and eyed the item of luggage with suspicion, trying to recall her relationship with this unexpected visitor. She put down the scoopful of dates, wiped her hands on a towel and looked again curiously at this woman.

Our visitor didn't wait to be recognized, but cheerfully addressed my mother "I'm Margaret. Margaret Mornington. We used to work together in Auckland a long time ago and now I've come to Sydney..." she smiled and nodded "yes, I've come all the way from New Zealand."

Mother did recall this acquaintance, and while she seemed pleased to see her, she was also concerned about where Margaret intended to stay, and for how long. I was sent into the house and for some time, the two women visited together in the shop, and finally arrangements were made for her stay.

Margaret dragged her large suitcase up to the

girls' bedroom and with a deep sigh, but still cheerfully smiling, sat on the bottom bunk, "Oh, this will do me nicely." And it did. Margaret Mornington lived with us for many months, was ever good-natured and helpful and inconspicuously slotted into our complicated household.

She shared our small bedroom with my two sisters and me, but was never in the way and thoughtfully made herself scarce whenever we were using the room. Quietly, she would slip into bed while we were asleep, and vacated and tidied her bunk by the time we were dressing for school. We grew used to seeing her attending to one of the children, helping out in the shop or doing the family wash.

Margaret was the most accommodating and cheerful person I had ever met and once she extended an extraordinary act of kindness to me. I needed a special dress for an important celebration at school at which I was to play the cello. Farmers, the large department store on Market Street in Sydney, had in their window, a red and white floral cotton dress edged in white eyelet. The price tag read one pound. I detoured by this store daily on my way home from the Conservatorium to gaze at this lovely garment which I was sure would make me beautiful, sophisticated and a great social success.

I nervously approached my mother, hoping that she might provide me with the money. Her reply was unreasonable to a thirteen year-old girl who wanted desperately to have, for once, a dress that was pretty and brand new, and not a hand-me-down from an older sister. Margaret found me weeping in our bedroom. She consoled me and without hesitation, took from her purse, a valuable one pound note, "I think it's important that you have this dress, and don't worry, I'll explain it to May." Her explanation must have been very good because Mother was only full of praise when I excitedly appeared in the becoming new dress.

We never knew why Margaret had come to Australia from New Zealand, but she told us that she was a writer, and indeed, as soon as we vacated our bedroom in the mornings, she would set up a little table and a noisy old typewriter that had been packed with her clothes in the large suitcase, and clatter away creatively. Under her bunk, she kept two cardboard boxes, one containing blank-paper, and the other, sheaves of typed pages. If we came into the room unexpectedly, she would smile, and moving her small table, excuse herself saying, "I'll just be a moment and get this out of your way, dear."

She often had at the foot of her bed, copies of a popular escapist magazine, *True Romances.* Pat and I would read them surreptitiously, hoping to find out more about "all that". But even to innocent schoolgirls, these stories carried little substantial information, though we nonetheless enjoyed the pages full of deep sighs, suggestive covert looks and dark brooding strangers standing in doorways. On one occasion, when Margaret had left many pages of her own writing on the table, we took the liberty of reading them and realized that she was writing love stories just like the ones we had read in *True Romances*. She immediately went up in our estimation – we were sharing our bedroom with a romance writer! Needless to say, our prying didn't stop there. The next step was to read all the typed pages in the box she kept under the bed. We took it in turns to read the stories, with one of us always stationed at the top of the stairs ready to signal at the approach of an adult.

By now, my father had grown weary of the morning clatter of what he always referred to as Margaret's "tripewriter". Having read the stories, Pat and I found this expression particularly humorous.

A day came when, with the arrival of the mail, Margaret's ready smile became absolutely radiant. She announced to the family that one of her stories had been published in *True Romances* and proudly waved the check that was enclosed in the envelope. We were all very happy for her except my father, who was appalled to discover that all this time "romance trash" was being written under his roof – and that he was the last to know.

However, it was this romance trash that liberated Margaret, and enabled her to move on from our cramped house. The large suitcase was re-packed with her clothes and tripewriter, and with a hug and a smile, she said her farewells to each of us. We missed her cheerful presence, her kindness – and our illicit reading of her romance stories.

BEXLEY NORTH

On August 9th, 1945, I was in class at the Conservatorium High School when our principal, Dr. Doris Coutts, announced to our small group of nine students that the Allied Forces were victorious in the Pacific and the War was now over. We were given the rest of the day as a holiday and told to go directly home, and to avoid the crowds which were expected to gather on the streets. She also suggested that it would be fitting to make a detour to the church of our choice and give thanks to God for the end to hostilities.

I quickly packed my school bag, and excitedly headed down Macquarie Street, which was already becoming noisy and crowded with jubilant workers leaving government offices and medical buildings.

St. Mary's Cathedral was fast filling with worshippers and ascending its sandstone steps, I entered the quiet darkened interior, which was illuminated only by candles and diffused coloured-light from the stain-glassed windows. St. Mary's had always offered a few moments of comfort and quiet on my way home from school, and on this historic day of peace, I knelt at a pew and gave thanks. Priests were already making preparations at the altar for Mass, and for a while I watched, but then became distracted by some of the people about me, and with sobering realization observed that many were not at all jubilant, but were openly weeping.

Stepping out into the brilliant Sydney sunshine and ignoring Dr. Coutts' directive "to go straight home", I ambled slowly through Hyde Park where a crowd of people were gathering by the reflection pool at the War Memorial. I took a long time to wend my way down to the ferry terminal.

The streets were now thick with revelers who, with unusual familiarity, embraced and danced about with whoever was closest to them, and with schoolgirl envy I observed laughing young women being swept up and twirled around by exuberant men who undoubtedly felt that their forwardness was justified by the military uniforms they wore. The ferry I boarded for the trip to Balmain blasted its horn incessantly, adding to the cacophony of sound generated by every other ferry, yacht and tugboat on the harbor.

For the rest of V-P Day, more than the usual number of customers were in and out of our shop, sharing their need to communicate with each other and to recount and judge events of the long years of war.

After dinner, Dad told us that there was to be a fireworks display in the city. As this was a unique occasion, we would all be allowed to sit outside on the shop awning which afforded a good view of the harbor skyline to watch the display, providing that we promised to sit at the very back, not go near the edges where we could fall to the street and for once, behave ourselves and not push and shove. It was such a special treat for us that we readily obeyed every instruction and were rewarded with our first magical display of exploding, luminescent fireworks.

The cessation of fighting in the Pacific brought an end to more than just the war. Within the next six months, my parents announced to us that they had purchased a house in a suburb I had never heard of before, Bexley North. We were unaware that they had even been house-hunting, although there was always much talk about someday moving their family out of Balmain, which at that time – in a British influenced, class conscious society – carried the stigma of being a "working-class" suburb. Also, the work and responsibility of a business, which my parents had operated for fifteen years, must have become increasingly arduous. But the sudden announcement that in the next few days we would be packing up our home and leaving Balmain still came as a shock to all of us.

* * *

On moving day, we left Balmain in the early morning for school armed with an address in Bexley North and the name of the nearest train station, Rockdale. Although I knew the city of Sydney very well, I had no experience with the trains and buses of the suburbs.

After school, I met Cathleen and together we walked to St. James railway station and purchased our tickets. Every time the train stopped, we anxiously checked the name posted at each unfamiliar station. It was a long thirty minute journey before we finally arrived at Rockdale. We then located our bus amongst the many double-deckers parked near the station and asked the driver to let us off at the nearest stop to Laycock Street. After alighting, we walked for a long time looking for our new house. It was dusk and the cold air had a sharp crispness to it that reminded us of our boarding school stay in Narellan.

The long, unpaved street was deserted and the few houses on it were surrounded by large tracts of empty, unkempt land, typical of many new suburbs whose expansion had been interrupted by the war. The footpath was overgrown with paspalam grass whose sticky seed heads clung to our legs and the hems of our uniforms. There were no shops where we could ask directions, and with no vehicles driving by, the quiet was unsettling. Soberly, we realized that we had virtually moved to the country.

When we finally arrived at 75 Laycock Street, we hesitated at the low, wooden front gate, tenuously taking in the first view of our new home. It was a single-storey free-standing house constructed with dark bricks which were popular in that era, of a color called "liver".

My brother Sean opened the front door, "What took you two so long to get here! We've been here for ages." Motioning us in, he exclaimed "Wait 'til you see everything, and we've got a big backyard now!"

Walking inquisitively from room to room, we couldn't experience Sean's same sense of excitement, but noted with dismay that our new house was not any larger nor had more rooms than the inner-city home we had just left. It offered three bedrooms and a verandah which we later enclosed. The kitchen was remarkably small and pokey, furnished with an old gas stove and a wooden table, and lit by a small window above the cast-iron sink. The house did have the advantage of a modern bathroom that boasted a gas-water heater rather than our previous one which burnt woodchips, and also an indoor toilet. Our modest furniture had been set up in the small living room, and on the dark oak picture rails, Dad had already hung his cherished collection of framed photos of Irish heroes.

In a time when we were totally dependent on public transportation, the selection of this house, located almost a mile walk from a station that only offered half-hour train service, didn't make sense to me. Even years later when the streets were paved and the empty lots of land filled with new homes, making the whole area look more suburban, Bexley North with its lack of transportation and shops, still remained inconvenient and lifeless. I can only presume that within my parents' budget, in this post-war period of severe housing shortages when in order to purchase a home, "key money" was handed over to the real estate agent, it was the best house available.

This move to the isolated suburbs had an unforeseeable affect on our family life, and on the spirit of my father and mother. Until now, with commitments at both high school and the Conservatorium, we would often make a couple of trips to the city each day and there was always one of us in and out of the house or running for a bus, tram or ferry, greeting my parents and customers as we came through the shop. Now that the journeys each way were so time-consuming, we were obliged to stay in the city more often, leaving early in the morning and sometimes catching the last train home at 11 P.M. Consequently, there was less sharing of meals, experiences and family events and although we still gathered to make music and sing, these times became more infrequent.

My father, after being his own boss for as long as I had known, now took a job in a government office, and dressed in a suit and hat with the obligatory newspaper tucked under his arm, became part of the workforce who took the crowded train in the early morning and late afternoon, commuting back and forth to the city centre. Because of his absence from the running of the household, and also his increasing health problems, Dad played a less dominant role in our lives, and now rarely had the opportunity to be what my mother good-naturedly referred to as, "The Great I-Am". However, the one area over which he was still able to maintain control over his increasingly independent family, was religion.

Leaving behind his former capricious relationship with the Church and his colourful interaction with engaging Irish priests, Dad now adopted, possibly with an awareness of his own mortality, an annoyingly conservative loyalty to Catholicism. Those of us who were home on Sunday nights were mustered into the living room to recite the Rosary. And he was now insistent that under no circumstances could Mass on Sunday be missed, despite the fact that our family had no history with this local parish, and instead of the comforting atmosphere and tradition of lovely old St. Augustine's in Balmain, we had to sit through dull services held in a temporary galvanized doorless shed that was an oven in the summer and a freezer in the winter. We obeyed him reluctantly.

In his political interests, Dad no longer promoted himself for local elections but did remain a member of the Labour Party, lending support to other candidates. Some of his former vital spirit would surface on election days when he would be very visible working the polling booths and promoting his candidate. If Labour won, Dad would volunteer a musical trio made up of his three daughters, to add to the festivities of the victory party.

The move to Bexley North also effected changes in my mother. Like my father, she had been well known in the community of Balmain, with her finger on the pulse of local activities. She was an interesting and social person, and running a business, even while attending to her large family, suited her energies well.

Now, with no identity in this new community, and no business to run, her children at school, and her husband away during the day, Mother was isolated at home with just my four year-old brother, Peadar, for company. But, never a person to indulge in complaining, she had a life habit of optimistically making the best of any situation.

Previously, she was surely often frustrated by the demands placed on her by family and the need to fulfill so many roles, so at first she took pleasure in having the time to be involved in many of the tasks that had always been the lot of her contemporaries.

Our home was now tidier which meant a lot to a frantic schoolgirl searching for a mislaid homework assignment or a missing belt to a school uniform before making a late dash for the morning train.

Mother was more available to arbitrate our constant battles over precious practice space, and solved some of these problems by assigning the unused garage as the practice area for my brothers, all of whom played brass instruments. This was helpful for the girls but must have been terrible for the neighbors, who by now, probably had reservations about the unconventional, noisy family next door. She took a new-found pleasure in having a yard, keeping a few chickens and growing plants, propagating them from small slips and cuttings that she set out in pots.

We were now expected to give a more specific accounting of our movements than we had previously and to tell mother when we would be home for dinner. Often when walking home from the train station, as we came over the crest of the hill past the empty lots, we could see mother standing on the verandah watching out for us. Then her figure would disappear into the house and shortly after we arrived home, our hot dinner would be ready and on the table.

But all of these diversions could only occupy this vital woman for just so long. By the time her youngest child was in school all day, mother knew the train time tables and the routes of our newly-installed bus service very well. She now had the freedom to visit old friends in Balmain and to enjoy some of the activities offered in the city. Sometimes she made the trip to Oxford Street to visit old Danny Boy for a "long chat and a ha'porth the apples," an Irish expression which referred to spending a long time with the shopkeeper but not spending much money.

Then one day, home unusually early, I looked out towards the crest of the hill and saw Mother appear, walking from the station. I put the kettle on for tea and went out to relieve her of the groceries she carried. Even after the long walk, there was a spring in her step and a glow of satisfaction on her face, and as she greeted me, I saw that she clutched in her right hand a familiar old black Gladstone bag.

THE OPPOSITE SEX

Because I attended the Conservatorium, and also its co-ed high school, I had, at fifteen, sufficient opportunity to mix with members of the opposite sex. My friends and I would frequently meet at each other's houses and spend an afternoon or an evening playing music.

We often met at my house and my parents always welcomed visitors and approved of us socializing in groups. But they had an innate suspicion of any situation that could lead to one-on-one dating, and, always ready to spot a potential romance, were equally ready to put a stop to it. I had different ideas... but my embarkment into the sophisticated world of dating was not one of great success.

My older sisters' quashed attempts to date made a strong impression on me. If their request to go on a date wasn't met with outright refusal by my parents, then at least circumstances were made sufficiently unpleasant that future dates weren't mentioned.

Maureen with her sisters Cathleen and Patricia.

On one occasion, Cathleen was invited to a concert by a young man, and intending to offer him coffee after he saw her home, she asked me to "take down the heroes". These were the large, framed photos of martyred Irish men that dominated the walls of our living room. Centred at the bottom of each photo was a placard and inscribed in India Ink with fine calligraphy, was the name, birth and death dates of each man, and finally, the contentious statement, "Murdered By The British". Needless to say, in our teen years when we wanted to be conformist, these imposing wall furnishings were of great embarrassment to us.

During the evening, I removed the cumbersome

frames from the walls and stacked them neatly behind the couch. This activity could not have gone unnoticed, but any comment was reserved until Cathleen had arrived home and was visiting with her date in the living room. Then my father, on the pretense of needing some forgotten item, barged in, and with mock surprise, looked around at the naked walls and exclaimed "Where are my pictures?! Where are the heroes!" Then, much to my sister's mortification, he busied himself retrieving and re-hanging them, all the time dissertating on their history to her captive date.

So with adolescent wisdom, I kept my first solo invitation a secret. This date was with an older voice student at the Conservatorium who had invited me to see an afternoon showing of *Waterloo Bridge* at the Minerva Theater. I knew it was a date because he paid for my ticket. Although my companion left little impression, what made the occasion memorable was the enrichment of my vocabulary by the word "naive". I understood its meaning but had always read it as "nave", so at the dramatic moment when Vivien Leigh announced "Oh Lady Margaret, you ARE NAI-EVE", a whole new world of sophisticated speech opened up to me.

For weeks, I used this word ad nauseam, stretching the syllables out in the most pompous-sounding fashion, until one evening at the dinner table, when I turned to my brother Sean, and said "You are SO NAI-EEE-VE!"

My father thumped the ladle down on the table and declared menacingly, "If I hear that snobby word from you once more, you will regret ever having used it!"

But surely a social experience with a male could enrich my life with more than just one single, forbidden word. So the next time a young man asked me to the pictures, I was again receptive.

My sister Pat and I had discovered that in Canterbury, a neighboring suburb of Bexley North, on the first Saturday night of each month, the local Parents & Citizens Association held social dances for young people. We were forbidden to attend dances, a restriction which I never understood, because my mother had loved going to socials as a young woman and indeed was a very good dancer. So although these chaperoned gatherings were innocent, we decided it was judicious to tell our parents that we were going to a concert rather than a dance. We attended several of these "concerts".

Decorated with crepe paper streamers and brightly lit, the Canterbury Community Hall was, on these Saturday nights, a noisy, exciting hub of youthful energy. The young men, outfitted in their good suits, congregated on one side of the hall, many lounging against the wall assuming an indifferent air. At the other end of the hall, were the girls – teenage hopefuls dressed up in colourful party frocks, the most resplendent of which were decorated with a sophisticated posy of silk flowers.

The girls' side of the room was always noisy, the chattering often punctuated with shrill, nervous giggles. The spectrum of colour was constantly moving as they scampered back and forth or temporarily left to visit the ladies room to check that their vibrant lipstick was still on their lips and not on their teeth, and to coax one more bounce from a wilting curl.

On the stage was a trio of musicians, led by the pianist, a large woman with marcelled grey hair, who wore a floor length crepe gown in a shade popularly known as "dusty pink". Attached to the right shoulder of her dress was an enormous satin bow that bounced in rhythm with her right hand as she thumped out the melodies on an old upright piano. Two balding, diminutive men, who could have been twins, completed the trio. One scraped away at the lead tune on his violin, and the other sat with eyes closed, brushing the same rhythm from a drum set all night.

The evening's dancing was always declared open with the announcement "Ladies and Gentlemen, take your partners for The Barn Dance."

I was often invited to dance by a good-looking, serious young man, and so it was that I got to know Bruce. After several Saturdays of executing waltzes and fox trots with him, and being gallantly accompanied to the bus stop with my sister after the dance, Bruce asked if he could take me to the pictures the following Saturday night. Flattered and excited at the prospect of being called for and escorted by a handsome young man, I agreed. But as the week progressed and I still hadn't plucked up the courage to ask my parent's permission, my enthusiasm paled.

Cancellation was out of the question as phone numbers hadn't even been exchanged. All day Saturday I made myself suspiciously useful, dedicated to being a helpful daughter.

Bruce was due to arrive at the house at six. At five o'clock, I nervously mumbled to my mother, "Can I go out tonight?"

She questioned me, "Go where?"

The mumbling continued, "I want to go to the pictures – with a boy."

Four little words can strike such terror – "WHAT DID YOU SAY??"

I stopped mumbling and looked honestly at my mother. "I have been invited to the pictures tonight and Bruce will be here in an hour and I want to go."

Mother had this frightening way of talking without addressing me but I was completely aware that every word, while not directed at me, was definitely aimed at me.

"Ah, this is nice, this is. I knew when you hung around all day helping out that there was something in the wind that wasn't in the weather." Her diatribe continued, and the inevitable phrase "After all I've done for you!" studded every sentence. It was drawn to my attention that great sacrifices had been made to educate me so that I could have a fine career in music.

"What chance do you think you'll have if you give it all up for the first man who comes along!" she exclaimed, echoing the frustrations of her own youth. To her daughters, she had often expressed resentment towards a society that expected young women to sacrifice the three R's of education for the three R's of marriage: Redemption, Respectability and Repression.

She finally looked at me and fired her questions. "Who is this boy and where does he come from? How old is he? What does he do for a living?"

By now I was weeping. "His name is Bruce, he's a very nice boy and he's a printer's apprentice."

It took a moment of suspenseful silence for all of my mother's snobbery to bubble to the surface. Then she erupted "Oh, so now the best you can do is to go out with tradesmen."

I screamed back at her "I'm not going out with men! I've only been asked to go to one picture show by one boy!"

My father entered the house at this stage of the argument. "What on earth is going on? You can be heard halfway down the street!"

With forced calm, my mother turned to him "Oh nothing's going on. It's just your youngest daughter. SHE wants nothing better than to gallivant all over the city with tradesmen."

This time the four words were explosive.

"WHAT DID YOU SAY??"

Rows in our household were never private. We didn't have the luxury of extra space, so often to our embarrassment, the details of arguments were shared by neighbors, and the rest of the family, listening and mentally taking sides, formed a mute audience. But this time everybody had something to say. My brothers and sisters sided with me, interjecting "Maureen didn't do anything wrong, she only wants to go to the pictures with a friend."

Maintaining their usual united front, my parents reinforced each other's opinion that I was ungrateful, lazy, arrogant, and unmotivated.

Between sobs, I tried to defend myself, finally turning to my mother and crying "I only asked to go to the pictures with a boy. You were practically MARRIED at my age."

"Yes, but I didn't have anything better" she

blurted.

Instantly, an ominous silence reigned and we all felt the focus of attention in the room shift. Dad fixed on Mother a look of fury. "So, you didn't have anything better, eh?"

Her unfortunate remark was irretrievable and for the next half-hour, they re-lived every less desirable incident from their marriage. But at least I was off the hook.

Then my father's acrimonious tone changed, as did his tack, and artfully addressing my mother, he inquired "And what's wrong with one of my daughters going to the pictures with a nice boy? Can you tell me that?" He continued to needle her, "Are my girls not attractive enough to be asked out?"

My father turned to me with benevolent paternalism "Of course you can go to the pictures with your young man."

My victory was hollow. By now, I dreaded having to go. My eyes were swollen and my body was wracked by the legacy of incessant crying – uncontrollable hiccups.

The unsuspecting Bruce was due to arrive in five minutes and the house quickly became a hive of solicitous activity. My sisters hurriedly helped me into my dress, brushed my hair and optimistically patted my tear-blotched face with a powder puff. My brother Seamus gave my shoes a quick polish. Everybody wanted to help.

The doorbell rang and a hush fell on the house. I heard my mother answer it and graciously say "You must be Bruce. Won't you come in." I couldn't believe it.

Dressed in his best brown suit, Bruce was escorted into the living room and introduced to my father. The worst was yet to come. I heard Dad, his voice resonating through the house, extend greetings and then inquire "And what are your intentions towards my daughter?"

Startled, Bruce answer him "Well Sir, I just want to take her to the pictures. I'll bring her straight home afterwards."

Mother, with a honeyed voice, then called me from the bedroom "Maureen, Bruce is here. Now you don't want to be late for the pictures."

We walked the half mile to Kingsgrove Theatre and exchanged not one word all the way. Bruce purchased and handed me the obligatory half-pound box of Nestle's Winning Post Chocolates. My body was still wrenched by loud hiccups which continued throughout the movie.

We walked home, again in silence, and at the door he thanked me for a lovely evening and I never saw him again.

I stopped going to the Canterbury dances and

about six months later, mother unexpectedly turned to me and inquired "Whatever happened to that nice young man who took you to the pictures?"

TRUE ROMANCE

After my mother's initial resistance, she accepted that I would go out on dates. My first real boyfriend was a man of twenty-one who was a student at the University of Sydney and also attended the Conservatorium for oboe lessons. Simon Peck, we shall call him, was tall and thin, smoked a Meerschaum pipe, wore a deerstalker on his head, assumed a British accent – and was a terrible snob. However, at sixteen, I was charmed by his "worldliness" and considered him very sophisticated.

Simon introduced me to the world of foreign films and insisted that I read D.H. Lawrence. He assured me that sophisticated women NEVER used sugar in tea or coffee so I immediately discarded the family custom of stirring at least three spoonfuls into my cup. Once, he even took me to dinner at a Chinese restaurant by Circular Quay known as the "Dirty and Plenty". He ordered for himself an exotic Asian dish known as "Fried Rice" but dismissed my attempt to order by informing the waitress, "She doesn't want to eat. She's too fat so just bring her tea."

Despite such displays of chivalry, our friendship lasted more than a year, but didn't survive an incident which occurred after my mother tried to be helpful.

Simon had invited me to afternoon tea at his parents' home on the North Shore. Having been told how his mother was very proper and his house was so elegant, I became increasingly anxious about the visit. I examined my meager wardrobe for something suitable to wear on this occasion and discussed the problem with my mother who suggested "What's wrong with your black velvet?" My black velvet, which had originally belonged to Cathleen, had been renovated many times to change its style and to give the impression that it was part of an extensive wardrobe. A lace collar had been added, then the neckline had been squared and bound in ribbon to match a new pink sash, and finally, during one of my growth spurts, a deep frill of tartan taffeta had lengthened it.

"What's wrong with it? It's a shabby mess. Maybe it would look alright if I could take it to the drycleaners to be spruced up."

"Oh you don't need to spend money like that" mother replied helpfully. "When I was a girl, we dry-cleaned our clothes by washing them in kerosene." This was a new one on me.

"But surely that would make it smell."

"Oh no" mother reassured me. "After you wash

your dress, hang it out on the line for the day to dry and air and it will be just like new."

We had a tin of kerosene in the laundry and after pouring the contents of it into the basin, I dunked my versatile dress up and down in it, averting my head to escape the fumes, and then hung the dripping garment on the line. And indeed, when it was dry, it looked very fresh and clean and no kerosene odor could be detected.

Feeling pretty and confident, I caught the train and found my way to Simon's house. It was a cold afternoon and after introductions, Mr. Peck invited me to make myself comfortable in a seat by the fire. From a coffee table invitingly spread with dainty cakes and sandwiches, Mrs. Peck served me my selection on a floral china plate. Everything went well at first. I accepted my cup of tea, with milk, no sugar thank you, and nibbled on a small pastry answering the polite questions put to me by Simon's parents.

During a lull in the conversation, I noticed Mrs. Peck looking quizzical, and when she wrinkled her nose in a sniffing gesture, I knew, with a sense of doom, that my cleaned dress was betraying me. She turned to her husband "Dear, I believe I can smell petrol."

Exposed to the warmth of the open fire, the black velvet emitted an increasingly strong odor of kerosene which quickly permeated the enclosed room. Mr. Peck, nostrils dilated, got up from his chair. "Yes, I believe there is an oil smell, isn't there. What could it be?" Reaching for his cardigan, he turned to Simon "Let's go and check the car."

Father and son went outside and I was left alone with Mrs. Peck. Too embarrassed to look at her, I gingerly squirmed about in the large chair, hoping in some way, to distance myself and the offending dress from the heat of the fireplace.

Simon returned and unwittingly rescued me, "Well the car seems okay. In any case, Maureen, it's getting late so I had better take you to the train."

My exit into the fresh air was swift and enthusiastic, but as Simon drove me to the station, he exclaimed in a puzzled voice, "This is insane. Now the oil smell is stronger than ever. There MUST be something wrong with the car!"

"No Simon, it isn't the car." I gulped and took a deep breath - "It's my dress."

He peered at me around the steering wheel "What are you talking about?"

Now that I had escaped the presence of his parents, my confidence started to return and I hesitantly explained the failed cleaning process my dress had undergone, hoping that he would be understanding. I was wrong. The action I had taken and my mother's advice appalled him. "But you could have even combusted – right in my parent's living room!"

Having been so preoccupied with the embarrassment of the situation, this possibility had not even occurred to me, but the mental picture it immediately conjured up made me start to giggle. Simon became all the more exasperated, "I simply can't understand how you could do such a thing. How am I ever going to explain such bizarre behavior to my parents?!"

He droned on with his peevish complaints all the way to the station. By the time we arrived, I realized that Simon Peck, my worldly, sophisticated older man, was really a humourless, selfish bore.

MOTHERS & DAUGHTERS

At seventeen, I now knew without any doubt that to play the cello and make music my career, was the most important element of my life.

The Conservatorium had been my second home since I was a small child, the place where I had spent my high school years, and now as a more advanced student of cello, where I continued my studies. There, I also made the contacts for semi-professional engagements in orchestras and chamber groups that provided me with experience, token amounts of pocket money and subsequently, a more "grown up" social life.

I acquired small sophistications. "Dare you wear Forbidden Fruit?" challenged the advertisements for a new line of lipstick. The payment from a music club performance gave me the opportunity to Dare, but when I tubed the cherry-coloured compound on my lips, I was rebuked by my mother for "looking tarty", so I postponed my glorification until I reached the privacy of the train station. In the mirrorless waiting room, I assumed a determined pout and outlined my lips in carmine, following their edges as though reading

Braille.

Now when the Conservatorium Orchestra sessions ended in the evening, I joined other older students at the Mocambo Coffee Shop, carrying my cello, and armed with my two important social tools – the tube of Forbidden Fruit, and sixpence for the cup of coffee which justified my occupation of a seat in this popular café. When the menu was circulated, I usually glanced at it casually, reading it from right to left, before I passed it on declaring in a world-weary voice "Nothing for me thanks, I'm not really hungry."

I used a similar ploy when the impatient waitress encouraged us to invest in another cup of coffee - "I really can't. Much as I love coffee, I would suffer from insomnia."

The truth was, a brass band would not have woken me from the limited amounts of sleep that I now had.

So with my precious sixpence well-invested in the enhancement of my social and intellectual life, I would leave the stimulating company of friends in the smoky coffee shop to catch the last train home, and after the long and lonely walk from the station, I would arrive at our house hungry and tired, but was always heartened when my mother called out from the bedroom, "Is that you, Love?"

I was seldom home now for family meals, so

when Mother joined me in the kitchen late at night, to quickly fry me a chop or a couple of eggs, her company and patient silence was reassuring. While I ate, she would prepare a pot of tea for us to share. She would pour a little milk in both of our cups, filling them then with tea. And while sipping the strong, hot liquid, we would share some of the day's experiences, talking softly. At times we sat silently, each absorbing the presence of the other, with the unconscious sense of the limited remaining time to be together that must have, on similar occasions, filtered into the minds of generations of mothers and daughters.

❊ ❊ ❊

I sat in the Green Room of the Sydney Opera House, and watched as my teen-aged daughter walked towards me across the thickly carpeted floor, carrying her cello, and wearing the grey uniform of the Conservatorium High School.

I had not returned to Sydney after six months in New Zealand as my cello teacher suggested, but played in the National Orchestra for two years. Then I traveled to the United States for further study and continued playing in many professional orchestras, until, completing the journey I had begun 25 years previously, I returned to Sydney with three school-aged children, accepting a position as cellist in the Sydney Symphony Orchestra.

When I had attended the concerts of the Sydney Symphony as a student, they were held in the Town Hall, an ornate Victorian sandstone structure next to St. Andrew's Cathedral on George Street. Now, while some subscription series were still held there, home for the orchestra was the stunning and unique Opera House fronting Sydney Harbour. Touring with various orchestras in the United States, I had become familiar with backstage areas of many concert halls, and thought wryly that even some of the most famous of them – Carnegie Hall in New York, the Academy of Music in Philadelphia, Lyric Theatre in Chicago – couldn't approach the luxurious facilities available to the musicians, singers, actors and dancers at the Sydney Opera House.

My daughter hadn't yet noticed me so I remained seated in the comfortable armchair casually observing her. She had stopped to greet two members of the cello section of the orchestra, and was now engaged in conversation with them, smiling shyly. Her right hand was in the pocket of her school blazer, her fingers pushing the seam to its limit. I too had worn such a blazer with its pocket crest of *Fiat Lux* (*Let There Be Light*) many years ago when I had attended this same school, as had five of my sisters and brothers.

The turreted building that housed the Conservatorium and the tiny high school was surrounded by the Botanical Gardens and had originally been the stables of Government House. In 1926, it had been converted to its present use.

The school was larger and more structured now. When I had attended, our class of nine students – six girls, three boys – had many lessons in the Botanical Gardens, because only two classrooms were available to the entire school of five years – fifty students in all.

It was only many years later that I fully realized how fortunate I was to have had the unique situation of being one of a very small group of high school music students, who met for classes in the summer house of the rose garden. What a challenge we must have been to our teachers!

We, who decided that the best position for study was lying on our stomachs, supporting our chins on arms crossed in front of us, stretched out on the soft lawns between the cultivated beds of perfumed blooms. And we, who were more likely to concentrate on the passage of an insect through the blades of grass, or the formation of a pillowed cloud in the clear blue sky overhead, than what our teachers were trying to instill in our resistant, juvenile heads.

But what wonderful teachers they were! Dr. Doris Coutts, who quietly tried to tame us with her constant example of the power of good manners, instill in us a love and understanding of the English language, and attempted to teach us the timelessness and universality of Shakespeare.

We had Livingstone Mote, who had also taught at the Conservatorium in the era of my sister and brother, fifteen years earlier. He was assigned to teach us French and Music History. Wearing his chalk-smudged black alpaca jacket, he would meet us for class - but now stooped and grey, rather than endure our rambunctious behavior, was just as likely to mumble "There's a rehearsal of Carmen in the Big Hall going on. Why don't you all go in there and see if Bizet doesn't do you as much good as learning French verbs does."

And, of course, we had, as did so many young budding musicians who followed in our footsteps, Betsy Brown. Miss Brown, a tiny, birdlike dynamo, who instructed us in Math, Geography, and Art, and in the study of this subject she constantly used the word "perspective". Indeed her insistence on our use of this evaluation was not limited to the study of Art.

She was the most feared of our teachers because

we knew that we couldn't hoodwink her. Despite her maturity, she hadn't forgotten how children think, and with her rapier tongue could put us in our place with one word or remark. "Bosh!" or "Stuff and nonsense!" she would exclaim, stripping away the veneer of our tales.

Miss Brown devoted her life to teaching young people and in training them to stretch their minds. But when she tried to train us to stretch our bodies, initiating a long overdue course in physical education at the school, she met resistance from music professors at the Conservatorium who worried that their students would hurt their hands. She countered by stitching soft bean bags for us to throw about, and taught us Morris Dancing and the use of the Maypole. So while in the more orthodox schools in Sydney, students were strengthening their bodies playing football and tennis, and lunging to a gymnastic pulse, we cavorted in the Botanical Gardens on the lawns at Farm Cove where the First Settlement in Australia had occurred, and under the tutelage of Betsy Brown and accompanied by a violinist from our class, we laughed freely and executed dances from a land and era when our own land was yet unknown.

Miss Brown maintained correspondence with her former students for decades, her "exes" as she called them. In conversation she placed them all chronologically, "So and so in London, he was after you, but before so and so", and we all had the honor of receiving regular correspondence from this wonderful lady, always penned in fine meticulous script.

Now as I sat reminiscing, I thought of one of the moving forces in the development of the Opera House, Sir Eugene Goossens. He was Director at the Conservatorium when I was a schoolgirl, and brought to the post his high standards and a long tradition of music making. He was my introduction to the music of Debussy, conducting the Conservatorium Opera Company and Orchestra in performances of *Pelleas et Melisande*. In rehearsal, he tried to project to us, his students - who were more comfortable with the loud multi-note difficulties of Wagner overtures than this ethereal impressionist music with its expanded rhythms – his love of Debussy's work, how it had influenced his own composing and how as a young student, he had lined up for a ticket to Debussy's London debut.

My daughter saw me, and her enthusiastic wave interrupted my reverie. She liked meeting me backstage, enjoying the glamourous atmosphere and the chance to see famous artists. We most usually took this opportunity to lunch together and there was the added bonus of a ride home with me, rather than having to take the train. I most often drove home now, not arriving by taxi, as I had promised myself as a child, but I had fulfilled many of my other childhood ambitions and did indeed, play on the stage in evening wear as my sisters and brothers had.

My daughter put her cello down next to mine and we placed the twin instruments, rigidly protected in their black cases, behind the armchair out of harm's way, while we purchased our lunch.

I poured our cups of tea and my daughter removed the sandwiches from the white plastic trays, and with schoolgirl appetite, she consumed the ham and salad sandwich, finishing her meal with the cup of strong tea, hesitating at one point to remove with her forefinger a cylindrical tea leaf that floated on the top.

I watched this action and was again beset by memories. How often had I sat with my own mother drinking tea, and when I had finished, she would reach across for my cup and with the hand that had effected this same movement for decades, swirled it around three times, depositing the last few drops of liquid in the saucer. Then holding the cup by its handle, its cavity facing her, she would bring it close to her, then move it away again, focusing on the few tea leaves that, having escaped the original straining when the hot tea was poured, now were stranded on the china surface, some flat and tiny, others cylindrical.

Years of watching this ritual had taught me not to interrupt my mother, but to wait patiently for any volunteered information. One late night when I was seventeen, she had read my tea cup "A letter – an important letter – is on its way to you."

The letter arrived on Monday. It was addressed to me but as the beige-coloured enveloped was typed and very official-looking with an overseas airmail stamp...

EPILOGUE

After playing in the New Zealand National Orchestra in Auckland, Maureen travelled to the United States and performed in New York with artists including Frank Sinatra and the orchestra of Radio City Music Hall and Mitch Miller.

She toured with Arthur Fiedler and the Boston Pops, where for the entire tour maestro Fiedler called her "Murine" instead of Maureen, confessing to her at the end of the tour that he knew her real name but preferred calling her "Murine" as she was easy on the eyes.

Maureen continued her music studies at the University of Miami and performed regularly at the famed Fontainebleau Hotel with the crooner Tony Martin.

In 1957, she was accepted into the New Orleans Symphony Orchestra, where she met and later married the principal cellist Barton Frank.

She also performed in the Seattle Symphony, various chamber orchestras, as a soloist and as a recording artist.

In 1974, Maureen returned to Australia as a single mother with three children. She played a blind audition behind a curtain (to avoid gender discrimination) and was accepted into the Sydney Symphony Orchestra.

During her career, Maureen performed with some of the world's musical greats including Dame Joan Sutherland, Aaron Copeland, Cleo Laine, Barry Tuckwell, John Dankworth, Charles Mackerras, Glenn Gould, Paul Tortelier and Louis Fremaux. She would assert, though, that one of her favorite artists was the actor and musician Danny Kaye when he conducted the Sydney Symphony Orchestra. Besides his exceptional musicianship, Kaye's mischievous sense of humor appealed to her.

For one Sydney Symphony concert, Maureen wore the wrong outfit – an evening when women in the orchestra were to wear a white blouse and long black skirt.

Thinking it was a concert where women could wear their own choice, she turned up in a cream blouse and a green, floral wrap-around skirt. As it was too late to go back home, she walked up and down the aisles of the concert hall at the Sydney Opera House scanning audience members for someone wearing a long black skirt. She finally found one, a sullen-looking woman, who after much persuasion and cajoling, reluctantly agreed to switch skirts for the duration of the concert.

At another Sydney Symphony concert, Maureen's strong sense of Irish patriotism made its way onstage.

At a rehearsal, she noted that *Rule Britannia* was on the program.

She warned management that she refused to perform such a piece and during the concert, placed her cello down and marched off stage at the Opera House, only returning at its end. She kept her job.

50500798R00124